The

Garden

Year

Planner

Other Books by Anne Halpin

GREAT GARDENS FROM EVERYDAY PLANTS, Fireside, 1993

500 TERRIFIC IDEAS FOR GARDENING, Fireside, 1993

THE YEAR-ROUND VEGETABLE GARDENER, Summit Books, 1992

THE NAMING OF FLOWERS, Harper & Row, 1990

FOOLPROOF PLANTING, Rodale Press, 1990

THE YEAR-ROUND FLOWER GARDENER, Summit Books, 1989

THE WINDOW BOX BOOK, Simon & Schuster, 1989

The Garden Year Planner

Anne Halpin

A Perigee Book

Perigee Books
are published by
The Putnam Publishing Group
200 Madison Avenue
New York, NY 10016

Library of Congress Cataloging-in-Publication Data

Halpin, Anne Moyer.
        The garden year planner / by Anne Halpin.
            p.   cm.
        Includes bibliographical references and index.
        ISBN 0-399-51864-9 (acid-free paper)
        1. Gardening . 2. Gardening—United States. 3. Gardening—
    Calendars. 4. Gardening—United States—Calendars. 5. Gardening—
    Charts, diagrams, etc. 6. Gardening—United States—Charts,
    diagrams, etc. I. Title.
    SB453.H35 1994   93-30008 CIP
    635' .0973—dc20

Cover design by Lisa Amoroso
Cover illustration © by Peter Siu

Book design by H. Roberts Design

Printed in the United States of America
1 2 3 4 5 6 7 8 9 10

This book is printed on acid-free paper.
∞

Contents

Introduction

M̲ost gardeners have busy schedules. Many of us work full time, or have families to care for, or homes to keep up. Few of us have the luxury of spending the better part of our day in the garden, much as we might like to. Instead, our gardening time is sandwiched in between the other events of our hectic lives. It's so easy to lose track of what our plants need, especially if we grow many kinds of plants.

This book is intended to be a handy, quick-reference guide to help you remember what to do when in the garden. The listings in the monthly sections are just simple reminders about basic garden activities. Everyone's garden is different; you will probably not find listed everything you do in your garden, and there are undoubtedly also reminders that do not pertain to your particular garden. So take what you can use from the book, and I hope you will find it easier to keep up with the progress of the gardening year.

Here in the introduction, and in the introductions to each of the monthly sections, you will find information about many of the techniques recommended in the monthly sections. Additional tips can be found at the end of each monthly section. Because of space limitations this information is very basic. If you are new to gardening it can help you get started, and if you are just a bit rusty it may help clear up confusion, but for detailed information you will need to consult other books or a good gardening encyclopedia. (See Recommended Reading, page 90.)

About Hardiness Zones and Climates

The monthly guides in this book are organized according to United States Department of Agriculture Plant Hardiness Zones, which represent the most widely accepted (although imperfect) system for dividing the widely divergent geographic areas of the United States and Canada into climatic regions. The zones on the map are based on the average annual minimum temperatures occurring across the country. But it is important to recognize that variations of weather and climate exist within each zone, and you must learn to understand the particular climate where you live. Do not simply follow by rote the recommendations you will find in this book. Observing your garden and landscape over a period of years will enable you to adapt this garden timetable to suit the conditions in your garden. In the meantime, use this book as a general guide.

Climate is not as simple as a zone map makes it seem. For one thing, weather is different from year to year. The zone map is based on *average* conditions, but winters may be colder or less cold than normal, summers may be hotter or cooler, wetter or drier. Your local United States Department of Agriculture (USDA) County Cooperative Extension office can tell you the average date of the last spring frost in your area, but the last frost in any given year may come before or after that date. The first fall frost may arrive earlier or later than its average date. Gardeners need to be able to adjust to the vagaries of the weather, and we also have to decide whether we want to play it safe and work well within the usual boundaries of our weather, or take chances on planting earlier or growing plants of borderline hardiness.

Another important determinant of growing conditions is microclimate—the local conditions in and immediately around your garden. Hardiness zones are generalized, and conditions vary within them according to local factors. Conditions that can influence microclimate include elevation, slope, exposure, soil type, shelters and windbreaks, and the presence of large bodies of water.

Gardens at higher elevations are subject to more severe conditions than those closer to sea level. A south-facing slope will be warmer than one that faces north or east. A garden at the bottom of a hill will be colder than one farther up, because cold air tends to flow down a hill and collect in a "cold pocket" at the bottom. A garden on the very top of the hill will be exposed to the elements, with no protection from strong prevailing winds or storms. A windbreak would be helpful in such a location, as it would be in other exposed, windy places.

If your garden is in a sheltered spot, such as along the south-facing wall of your house, it will enjoy warmer than average conditions. Such a location would receive maximum sun exposure and protection from north winds, a combination that can produce growing conditions equivalent to those found a zone farther to the south; you will probably be able to grow things your neighbors can't. A large body of water, too, will moderate the environment. If you live near the ocean or a large lake, temperatures will warm up more slowly in spring, cool off more slowly in fall, and not swing as widely up and down in summer and winter as temperatures farther from the water. Soil, too, plays a role. Heavy clay soils are slower to warm in spring and slower to cool in fall; light, sandy soils warm faster in spring and cool more quickly in fall.

Understanding the microclimate in your garden will help you to make more informed plant choices, and to make better use of your growing season.

Using Phenology to Determine Safe Planting Dates

One of the most critical times in the gardening year, especially for gardeners in cold climates, is spring planting, when planting too early leads to death for tender seedlings, and planting too late wastes precious time. Although a timetable like the one in this book is a useful guide to when to plant, you can't always trust the calendar. A more reliable guide to deciding when it is safe to plant is phenology. Phenology is the study of events that happen in regular cycles in the lives of plants and animals. The life cycles of perennial plants in the landscape are closely related to temperature and day length, and you can use plants as natural indicators of when conditions are suitable for sowing or setting out various plants.

Perennial and woody plants usually do not start to grow until the weather is warm enough for them. In a cold, wet spring they will get a later start, and so should your garden plants. Native Americans taught the colonists in New England to plant their corn when the oak leaves were as big as a mouse's ear. That advice is still valid today.

Another reliable indicator plant that many gardeners use is the lilac. Lilacs are good indicators because their annual development is very regular and easy to observe and because they grow in most parts of the United States. When lilac leaves first begin to emerge from the bud scales which enclosed them, it is safe to plant cool-weather vegetables like peas and lettuce, and hardy annuals such as calendulas and bachelor's buttons. When lilacs are in full bloom, that is, when all of the flowers on 95 percent of the plant's flower clusters are fully open, it is time to plant tender, warm-weather plants such as tomatoes, basil, wax begonias, and summer bulbs.

Watching local lilacs will help you to turn this book's general timetables for planting, which are given in terms of months and zones, into specific planting times for your garden.

The Soil

Soil is the basis of the garden, and understanding your soil will make it easier for you to choose plants likely to do well in your garden, and to improve the quality of your soil to make it a better growing medium for the plants.

There are three primary soil types, determined by the kinds of particles that compose them.

Sandy soils contain a high percentage of sand. Because sand particles are large compared to other soil particles, sandy soils have a light, loose texture which makes them fast-draining and easy to dig. Sandy soils can be worked quite early in spring, since they do not hold much moisture and thus tend to thaw quickly, but they also dry out rapidly in summer. Nutrients pass through sandy soil quickly, and the soil may be of poor nutritional quality for plants.

Clay soils have a large proportion of clay particles, which are tiny and tightly packed together. As a result, clay soils are dense, heavy, and slow to drain. Although such soil may contain adequate nutrients, it dries out very slowly in spring, and may become compacted and waterlogged if not handled properly. The advantage of clay, besides its nutrient value, is that it needs less watering in summer.

The addition of organic matter, in the form of compost or other natural materials, can improve the quality of both sandy and clay soils. Organic matter gives a sandy soil more body, improves its ability to hold water, and contributes some nutritional value. Adding organic matter to clay soil lightens the texture (organic matter particles are larger than clay particles), helps aerate the soil, and improves drainage.

The ideal garden soil is loam, a mixture of sand, clay, and silt, with organic matter and minerals. Loamy soils are crumbly textured and a rich brown color; they drain well while still retaining adequate moisture for plants, and are naturally fertile.

pH

pH is a measure of soil's acidity or alkalinity. It is measured on a scale of 0 to 14, with 7.0 being neutral. Numbers below 7.0 indicate acidity, the lower the number meaning the higher the acidity; numbers above 7.0 indicate increasing degrees of alkalinity.

Most plants thrive in soil that is neutral to mildly acidic, although many are adaptable. Some plants have a decided preference for acid soil (azaleas, rhododendrons, and ericaceous plants) or for alkaline soil (such as gypsophila and dianthus). Some regional generalizations can be made about soil pH, although they are just generalizations. Soil in the woodland areas of the eastern United States is usually acidic, the southwestern deserts are largely alkaline, and midwestern prairie soils are often near neutral. But the only way to know your soil's pH is to get it tested.

A soil test can show the levels of nutrients and organic matter in your soil in addition to pH. It is a good idea to get the soil tested when you start a new garden or move to a new location. You can buy a do-it-yourself test kit at a local garden center (invest in a good one) or get soil tested through the local County Extension office. There are also private laboratories that do soil testing.

It is possible to adjust soil pH to a modest degree, but you should not plan on making major changes. To slightly lower pH, work in acidic materials such as sulfur or peat moss. To raise pH add lime or wood ashes.

The best way to improve soil overall is to work in lots of organic matter. Decomposing mulches add organic matter, and you can also incorporate livestock manure (do not use pet droppings), rock powders, fish meal, or plant debris. One of the best ways to add organic matter to soil is in the form of compost.

Compost can be made as simply as piling up fallen leaves and letting them decompose over time (the result is called leaf mold). But building a compost pile according to traditional guidelines will allow the ingredients to break down quickly and odorlessly. A properly made compost pile does not smell bad. Finished compost is brown and crumbly, with an earthy smell.

To make compost, start by placing some small branches on the ground, to allow air circulation under the heap. A pen or bin will keep the pile in one place, but is not mandatory. On top of the branches, put down a two- to four-inch layer of green plant debris, weeds that have not yet gone to seed, or household garbage (use vegetable peels, coffee grounds, and eggshells, but do not use meat products, fats, or oils). You can use fresh grass clippings, but only in a thin layer or mixed with other plant material. Two inches of grass clippings would turn slimy and smelly. Follow that layer with several inches of dry material: shredded leaves, straw, dead (but not diseased) plants, pine needles. Next comes one to two inches of livestock manure or soil. Repeat the layers, moistening each layer as you build—the material should be damp but not soggy. Turn the pile with a pitchfork once a week to mix the materials and keep the decomposition process going. Fork material from the outer edges of the pile into the hot center. Sprinkle with a hose if the pile seems dry. The compost should be ready to use in a month or two.

Preparing Soil for Planting

In climates where winters are cold, planting begins in spring when the soil is ready to work; that is, when it has dried out and warmed sufficiently after winter's freeze to allow seeds to germinate and plants to grow. To tell whether your soil is ready to work, scoop up a handful and squeeze it into a ball in your hand. When you open your fingers, if the ball of soil sticks together it is still too wet to work. Digging now could cause compaction. But if the soil ball crumbles apart, it is time to dig the garden.

The soil should be loose to at least a foot deep; two feet is better. For the best texture, you can double-dig. That involves removing the soil to the depth of a spade (about a foot), loosening the subsoil with a spading fork, and then replacing the topsoil. Double-digging is hard work, and many gardeners do not bother with it. Do be sure to dig and turn over your soil to a depth of at least a foot, or run a rotary tiller as deeply into the soil as it will go. Break up large clods and lumps, and remove stones. Finally, rake the surface smooth.

Fall is also a good time to work the soil. As parts of the garden are emptied, spread a one-inch layer of compost over the soil and dig or till it in. Fall is also the best time to incorporate rock powders and other organic materials that break down slowly. For plants that remain in the ground all year—herbaceous perennials, woody plants, and bulbs—a topdressing of compost works just as well.

Adding an inch of organic matter to the soil each year will keep it in excellent condition.

Soil Care in a Cold Frame

Caring for the soil in a cold frame is a bit different. A cold frame is a bottomless box with a "floor" of soil and a removable or hinged cover made of clear glass or Plexiglas. The cold frame provides a protected environment for plants, rather like a miniature greenhouse. It will be easiest to do the initial soil preparation before you put the cold frame in place.

If you want to put a cold frame in a location that is not now part of your garden, you will first have to remove the sod, a fairly arduous task. Mark out an area of the dimensions of the cold frame, using stakes and string. Push the blade of a spade or shovel vertically into the soil across the width of the area, then repeat the process about a spade's width away. Push the spade under the turf, more or less horizontally, and lift it up. Continue chopping and lifting patches of turf until the area is clear. Knock as much soil off the turves as you can, and put them upside down in the compost pile. Then prepare the soil as in the garden. After the cold frame has been installed, you can simply add a layer of compost for the first couple of years. About every third year, remove the top four or five inches of soil and replace it with good garden soil, or a mixture of compost and soil.

USDA Plant Hardiness Zone Map

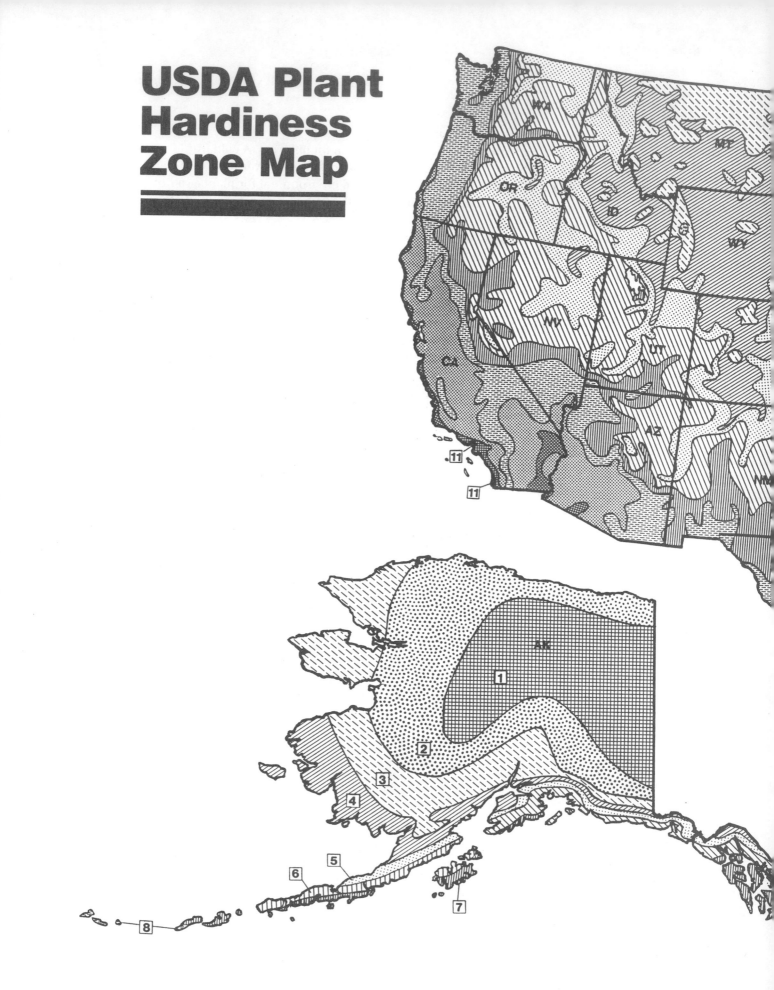

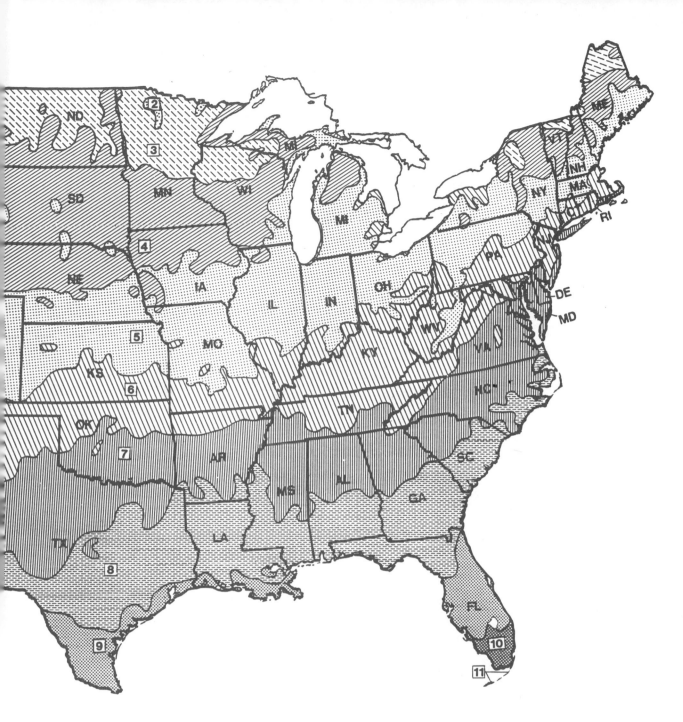

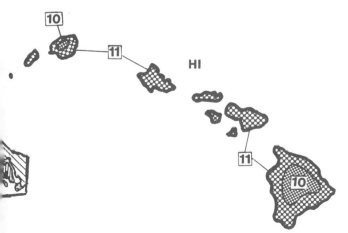

RANGE OF AVERAGE ANNUAL MINIMUM TEMPERATURES FOR EACH ZONE

ZONE 1	BELOW -50° F	
ZONE 2	-50° TO -40°	
ZONE 3	-40° TO -30°	
ZONE 4	-30° TO -20°	
ZONE 5	-20° TO -10°	
ZONE 6	-10° TO 0°	
ZONE 7	0° TO 10°	
ZONE 8	10° TO 20°	
ZONE 9	20° TO 30°	
ZONE 10	30° TO 40°	
ZONE 11	ABOVE 40°	

January

Designing a Garden

Winter is the best time to work on garden designs. If you have a garden that continues from year to year—a perennial bed or a shrub border, perhaps—you need only refine the design from year to year. If you want to start a new garden, this section should be of some help.

The first decision you must make is where to put the garden. For the widest choice of plants, look for a location in full sun that receives unobstructed sunlight for at least six hours a day. Light, dappled shade will also support a variety of plants, but avoid the deep shade cast by evergreens, heavily canopied shade trees, or a nearby building.

Avoid putting a garden in a low spot, where the soil is soggy when it rains, or a site at the bottom of a hill, where cold air will tend to collect. If your potential garden spot is in an exposed, windy place, plan on installing or planting a windbreak to shelter plants.

If your garden is to be ornamental—a flower bed or border—you should also consider how the new garden will relate to architectural features on the property, such as the house, garage, sidewalks, walls, and fences. The garden is for your enjoyment, so think about a location that will let you see the flowers from inside the house. Consider also what purpose you'd like the garden to serve. Will it be purely decorative? A place to read or play or entertain visitors in pleasant weather? Will the garden be devoted to the production of food or of flowers for cutting? Or would you like the garden to combine useful plants with an attractive design?

Gardens should relate in terms of scale and style to the rest of the property. At the same time, they should please your aesthetic sense and accommodate your life-style.

When you have found the right spot for the garden, the next step is to decide its form. Gardens come in many shapes and sizes. Very generally speaking, straight lines and geometric shapes convey a feeling of formality, while soft curves and irregular forms look more casual. You can plant shrubs in borders, in mixed hedgerows, as conventional hedges or screens, or as specimens in a lawn; Flowers—annuals, perennials, bulbs, or a blend of all three—can be gathered in borders (long, narrow gardens that define or divide different parts of the landscape), in beds of practically any size or shape, or in containers positioned individually or grouped on a porch, patio, deck, or rooftop. Vegetables can be grown by themselves, in rectangular, circular, or other geometrically shaped plots. Or you can grow edibles and ornamentals together in delightful profusion. Many vegetables and herbs are quite decorative in their own right, and incorporating them into ornamental gardens is a great space-saver for gardeners without lots of land.

Within the garden you can arrange plants in a number of ways. The most natural, appealing look for a flower garden is to plant in flowing, curved drifts of color. In very small gardens, plant in clumps of three, five, or seven of the same plant. If you prefer a controlled, very formal look, you can plant in precise squares, triangles, or other geometric patterns for an effect reminiscent of the elaborate carpet beds of the Victorian era. Bear in mind, however, that such gardens must be scrupulously maintained in order for their precise shapes to be appreciated.

Vegetables and herbs can be worked into either of these schemes, or you might opt for a more traditional garden planted in straight rows or blocks. Another option for edibles is to plant an old-fashioned kitchen garden, combining vegetables, herbs, small fruits, and edible flowers.

Whichever approach you take, try to plan for a gradation of heights so all the plants will be visible. That is, position the tallest plants in the back of the garden, with plants of medium height in front of them, shorter plants next, and low edging plants in the very front of the garden.

When designing the garden, consider what will be visible beyond it. You may want to create a backdrop for the garden to show off the plants to their best effect. A hedge or planting of conifers makes a lovely background for a flower garden. So does a stone wall or picket fence. If a less attractive feature, such as a chain-link fence, backs the garden, consider hiding it behind more plants. Ivy, morning glory, or another vine can handily cover an ugly fence. Or you could install lattice or trelliswork and train vines on it, or plant a living screen of hollyhocks, giant sunflowers, mixed shrubs, or other tall plants to camouflage the eyesore.

Another important issue in garden design is color. Choosing a color scheme for the garden will result in a more pleasing, coherent look. Even if you are growing vegetables, considering their color and form when deciding where to plant them will give you a more ornamental garden. There are several ways to work with color; which approach you choose depends on the kinds of colors you like. Do you prefer subtle, harmonious combinations of colors, or do you like contrasting colors? Do you like bright colors or pastels? Would a garden composed entirely of restful white flowers or shades and tints of a single color appeal to you, or would you rather see an exuberant mix of many hues?

Choosing one color to dominate the garden all season is the simplest approach. For example, if you like pink flowers you might have mountain pinks in early spring; pink tulips a bit later; columbines, bleeding heart, and hardy geranium in late spring and early summer; astilbe, spider flower, cosmos, petunias, and snapdragons in high summer; and pink asters in fall. A few purples or reds would add a nice accent.

To create a harmonious color scheme, mix colors that are related, or located close to one another on the kind of color wheel used by artists and decorators. Some examples of harmonious, or analogous, color combinations are pink, purple, and blue; red, orange, and gold; pink, rose, and lavender; and orange, bronze, and rusty red.

Contrasting colors are farther apart on the color wheel. The most intense contrast is created by complementary colors, which are opposites. When complementary colors are placed next to one another, the visual effect of both colors is intensified. Orange and blue are complements, as are yellow and violet, and red and green. If you want to use one of these intense combinations in your garden, you can soften the effect by using a pastel shade of one of the colors—yellow and lavender, for example. Another tactic would be to introduce some neutral tones into the garden—white flowers, or silver foliage, perhaps—or to add green foliage plants to absorb some of the color. Brightly contrasting colors are most satisfying to most viewers when they are seen from some distance rather than at close range. A garden vibrating with bright rose, orange, and purple could jangle the senses if it is packed into a tiny yard where viewers must stand right next to it. Of course, if a lively, stimulating effect is what you're after, strong color contrasts may be just what you need.

Another way to get a lot of visual activity into a garden is to use a multicolored, or polychromatic, scheme. Polychromatic gardens are often a chaotic jumble of hues, but many people like their brightness. English cottage gardens, with their happy riot of colors, are a good example of the polychromatic style. If you want lots of different colors without so much discord, try using all pastel shades instead of bold, strong tones.

Brush or sweep heavy snow from trees and shrubs, especially evergreens; let ice melt naturally.

Brush or sweep snow from trees and shrubs, especially evergreens; let ice melt naturally. Prune wisteria and other woody vines when weather permits from now till early spring. When temperature is 40 degrees F or above, spray broad-leaved evergreens with antidesiccant. Apply dormant oil sprays.

Remove heavy snow from trees and shrubs, especially evergreens. Prune trees, shrubs, and vines that bloom in summer or later, while dormant. When temperature is 40 degrees F or above, spray broad-leaved evergreens with antidesiccant. Fertilize acid-lovers.

See Zone 5

Plant bare-root trees and shrubs in pre-dug holes; stake if needed. Prune trees, shrubs, and vines that bloom in summer or later, while dormant. Fertilize acid-lovers if not done last fall.

Plant bare-root trees, shrubs, and vines while dormant. Prune summer and fall bloomers if not done last fall; prune evergreens and hedges while dormant. Fertilize acid-lovers if not done last fall. Water evergreens when soil thaws. In arid regions, water deciduous plants, desert trees, and shrubs. Watch for overwintering insects. Apply dormant oil spray when temperature is over 40 degrees F.

Plant bare-root stock while dormant, balled-and-burlapped and container-grown trees, shrubs, and vines when available locally. Prune summer and fall bloomers if not done last fall. Fertilize acid-lovers if not done last fall; feed new transplants with water-soluble fertilizer. Watch for overwintering insects. Apply dormant oil spray when temperature is over 40 degrees F. Layer shrubs.

Plant bare-root stock while dormant, balled-and-burlapped and container-grown trees, shrubs, and vines. Prune summer and fall bloomers if not done last fall. Fertilize acid-lovers if not done last fall; feed new transplants with water-soluble fertilizer. Water monthly if weather is dry. Layer shrubs.

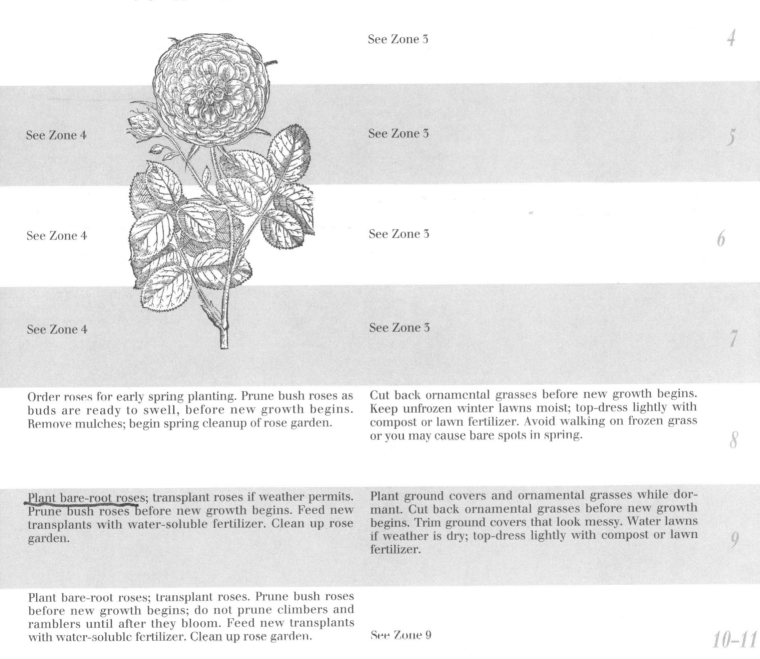

Use sand or ashes on icy walks and driveways—salt damages lawns and other plants. Avoid walking on frozen grass or you may cause bare spots in spring.

1–3

Order roses for early spring planting.

See Zone 3

4

See Zone 4

See Zone 3

5

See Zone 4

See Zone 3

6

See Zone 4

See Zone 3

7

Order roses for early spring planting. Prune bush roses as buds are ready to swell, before new growth begins. Remove mulches; begin spring cleanup of rose garden.

Cut back ornamental grasses before new growth begins. Keep unfrozen winter lawns moist; top-dress lightly with compost or lawn fertilizer. Avoid walking on frozen grass or you may cause bare spots in spring.

8

Plant bare-root roses; transplant roses if weather permits. Prune bush roses before new growth begins. Feed new transplants with water-soluble fertilizer. Clean up rose garden.

Plant ground covers and ornamental grasses while dormant. Cut back ornamental grasses before new growth begins. Trim ground covers that look messy. Water lawns if weather is dry; top-dress lightly with compost or lawn fertilizer.

9

Plant bare-root roses; transplant roses. Prune bush roses before new growth begins; do not prune climbers and ramblers until after they bloom. Feed new transplants with water-soluble fertilizer. Clean up rose garden.

See Zone 9

10–11

1-3

Prepare plant orders from mail-order sources. Periodically check winter protection in beds and borders.

4

Prepare plant orders from mail-order sources. Keep beds and borders mulched to prevent frost heaving. Gently press any heaved roots back into soil.

5

See Zone 4

If there is no snow cover, check mulches on bulb beds; replace if necessary. Check summer bulbs stored indoors; discard any with mold or rot; mist if starting to dry out.

6

Prepare plant orders from mail-order sources. Sow seeds indoors for transplanting out in spring. Check for slug damage to tender crowns; if present, sprinkle coarse sand and wood ashes around base of plants. Check for heaved roots; gently press back into soil. If soil is frozen, keep mulched.

When there is no snow cover, check mulches on bulb beds; replace if necessary. If spring bulbs emerge early, dust shoots with wood ashes to keep away slugs; mulch well. Check summer bulbs stored indoors; discard any with mold, rot, soft spots; mist if starting to dry out.

7

See Zone 6

As early bulbs begin to grow, sprinkle with wood ashes if slugs are a problem. Fertilize with bone meal or fertilizer. Check summer bulbs stored indoors; discard any with mold, rot, or soft spots; mist if starting to dry out.

8

Order plants for spring planting. Sow warm-weather perennials indoors. Mulch beds and borders with loose material. Cover marginally hardy plants if a freeze is expected. Fertilize perennials emerging from soil. Water as needed in arid Southwest; do not water cactus unless winter rainfall is below average.

See Zone 7

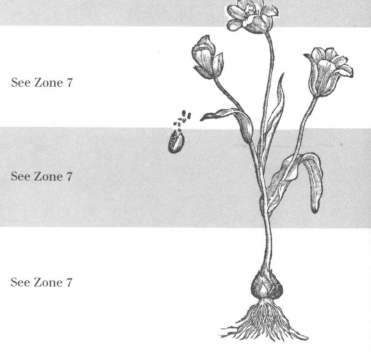

9

Order plants for spring planting. Sow warm-weather perennials indoors. Plant bare-root perennials while dormant. Fertilize perennials beginning to grow. Water new and established plants when needed. Cover marginally hardy plants if frost is expected. Begin spring cleanup of beds and borders.

See Zone 7

10-11

Order plants for spring planting. Sow warm-weather perennials indoors. Plant bare-root perennials while dormant. Fertilize perennials beginning to grow. Water new and established plants when needed. Begin spring cleanup of beds and borders.

See Zone 7

Annuals

Order seeds for spring planting. Care for indoor plants started from cuttings from last summer's garden.

Order seeds for spring planting. Start slow-growing annuals indoors. Care for indoor plants started from cuttings from last summer's garden.

See Zone 4

Order seeds for spring planting. Sow hardy annuals outdoors, even if ground is frozen. Start seeds of slow growers indoors. Care for indoor plants started from cuttings from last summer's garden.

Order seeds for spring planting. Sow hardy annuals outdoors, even if ground is frozen. In southern parts of zone, sow sweet peas in rich soil if ground is not frozen. Care for indoor plants started from cuttings from last summer's garden.

Order seeds for spring planting. Sow hardy annuals outdoors; sow sweet peas in rich soil. If you can grow winter annuals, fertilize them or top-dress with compost; water as needed. Care for indoor plants started from cuttings from last fall's garden.

Sow summer annuals indoors. Plant more hardy annuals outdoors. Fertilize outdoor annuals or top-dress with compost; water as needed; keep weeded. Clean up beds and borders. Deadhead winter annuals; remove worn-out plants. Take cuttings to start new plants.

Sow summer annuals indoors or in cold frame. Plant more hardy annuals outdoors. Fertilize outdoor annuals or top-dress with compost; water as needed; keep weeded. Clean up beds and borders. Deadhead winter annuals; remove worn-out plants. Take cuttings to start new plants.

	Container Gardens	Vegetables & Herbs
1-3	Begin cleaning out pots and containers to be planted in spring. Scrub out loose soil. Disinfect clay pots by soaking in bleach solution. Crush broken clay pots to use in bottom of containers when planting. Check tender container plants moved indoors for winter.	Plan successions and crop rotations for this year's garden. Test stored seeds for germination. Order new seeds. Be sure supplies are on hand for indoor seed-starting.
4	See Zone 3	Plan successions and crop rotations for this year's garden. Test stored seeds for germination. Order new seeds. Be sure supplies are on hand for indoor seed-starting. Sow onions and cabbage family indoors.
5	See Zone 3	Plan successions and crop rotations for this year's garden; update garden plans. Test stored seeds for germination. Be sure supplies are on hand for indoor seed-starting. Order new seeds. Sow onions and cabbage family indoors.
6	See Zone 3	See Zone 5

	Container Gardens	Vegetables & Herbs
7	Begin cleaning out pots and containers to be planted in spring. Scrub out loose soil and fertilizer salts. Disinfect clay pots by soaking in bleach solution. Crush broken clay pots to use in bottom of containers when planting. Inventory supplies; stock up for spring planting. Check tender container plants moved indoors for winter.	Finish updating garden plans. When soil conditions permit, direct-sow peas, early cabbage, spinach, lettuce; plant onion sets. Order new seeds.
8	Move outdoor container plants to protected spot in cold weather. Clean out pots and containers to be planted in spring. Scrub out loose soil and fertilizer salts. Disinfect clay pots with bleach solution. Crush broken clay pots to use in bottom of containers when planting. Inventory supplies; stock up for spring planting. Check tender container plants moved indoors for winter.	Prepare garden for planting; in Southwest, water well to flush out built-up salts. Direct-sow spinach and radishes. Sow other cool-season crops indoors or in cold frame to plant out next month. Plant asparagus roots.
9	Move outdoor container plants to protected spot in cold weather. Soak potted citrus trees to flush out excess fertilizer salts. Clean out pots and containers to be planted in spring. Scrub out loose soil and fertilizer salts. Disinfect clay pots with bleach solution. Crush broken clay pots to use in bottom of containers when planting. Inventory supplies; stock up for spring planting.	Prepare garden for planting; in Southwest, water well to flush out built-up salts. Direct-sow cool-season crops; sow summer vegetables and tender herbs in cold frame. Plant asparagus and artichoke roots. Fertilize crops already in garden.
10-11	Soak potted citrus trees to flush out excess fertilizer salts. Clean out pots and containers to be planted in spring. Scrub out loose soil and fertilizer salts. Disinfect clay pots to use in bottom of containers when planting. Inventory supplies; stock up for spring planting.	Prepare empty parts of garden for planting. Direct-sow cool-season crops; sow summer vegetables and tender herbs in cold frame. Plant asparagus and artichoke roots. Fertilize crops already in garden.

Fruit

Check tree guards and tree wraps. Order fruit for spring planting.

Check tree guards and tree wraps. Order fruit for spring planting. Sow alpine strawberries indoors. If temperature goes above 40 degrees F, prune apples, pears, and grapes from now till spring. If warmer than 40 degrees F for at least twenty-four hours, apply dormant oil sprays.

Order nursery stock for spring planting. Check tree guards, tree wraps, and mulches. Check stakes on fall-planted trees. On mild days, prune berries, brambles, grapes, trees. Also on mild days, check for overwintering pests; apply dormant oil sprays.

See Zone 5

See Zone 5

Plant bare-root nursery stock; plant strawberries. Prune berries, brambles, grapes, and trees. Fertilize established trees when growth begins. Check for overwintering pests; apply dormant oil sprays while trees are still dormant.

Plant bare-root nursery stock; plant strawberries. Prune deciduous trees, berries, and grapes. Fertilize established trees and strawberries. Check for overwintering pests; apply dormant oil sprays while trees are still dormant.

Plant bare-root nursery stock; plant strawberries. Prune deciduous trees, berries, and grapes. Fertilize established trees and strawberries. Check for overwintering pests; apply dormant oil sprays while trees are still dormant.

Design Tips

If you are not sure where to put a new garden, you could take some snapshots of your property. Have some enlargements made, and lay a piece of tracing paper or acetate on top of each one. Draw in the outline of a garden in a likely spot. Try to imagine how the garden would look with different kinds of plants—small trees, shrubs, flowers, vines, ground covers, or a combination of all those types. If you don't think you would like a garden in that place, take a new sheet of paper or acetate and try another location. Keep experimenting until you find a position you like.

When you have chosen a location for the garden, go outdoors to the intended location and lay out a rope, or lengths of garden hose, on the lawn in a shape you think you would like. Adjust the shape until it suits you. Then try out your ideas on paper before you start to dig.

Make a drawing of the potential garden and how you'd like to arrange groups of plants within it. The sketch can be a simple map as long as it allows you to try out your ideas. When you arrive at a final design, draw up a final sketch and label all the plantings so you will remember where you want to put the plants when you buy them. It is all too easy to forget.

If you are new to gardening, make your first garden small and simple. You can always expand it next year.

Don't be afraid to follow your instincts. Above all, your garden must please you. If you disagree with the rules set forth by gardening experts, make your own rules. Your garden should express your personality, not that of a designer whose book you've read.

If you will be growing flowers, try to plan for a succession of bloom. Many annuals bloom all season long, and they offer a good means of experimenting with different color schemes until you feel comfortable mixing and matching colors. In subsequent years, you can begin introducing perennials in combination with annuals, gradually expanding your range each year.

Let your garden evolve. It won't be perfect the first year. Don't be afraid to change next year what you don't like this year. Gardens are not static—they are ever-changing, and that is part of their appeal.

February

Starting Seeds Indoors

A great way to get a head start on the gardening season, especially for gardeners in cold climates where the outdoor growing season is brief, is to start seeds indoors. Indoor sowing for spring planting can begin anytime from January to April, depending on where you live and what you are planting. Some plants, such as sweet peas and squash, are difficult to transplant and are best sown directly in the garden. But many plants transplant easily, and you can gain weeks of outdoor growing time by starting them indoors.

Gardeners in the North benefit from starting tender, warm-season annuals, herbs, and vegetables indoors, to get a jump on spring. Gardeners in warm climates more often find it helpful to start seeds for the fall and winter garden indoors, out of the intense summer heat.

Containers for starting seeds must be clean—sterile, if possible, because young seedlings have little resistance to disease—and they should have drainage holes in the bottom. Practically any container meeting those requirements will work. You can use plastic cell packs (also called market packs or six packs), nursery flats, peat pots, peat pellets or cubes, boxes made of pressed wood fiber, clay or plastic flowerpots, margarine cups, Styrofoam beverage cups—whatever you prefer or happen to have on hand. If you will be starting large numbers of seeds, you will probably find it most convenient to use cell packs or small peat pots, and plant each seed in its own container. That will eliminate the need to thin or transplant before the seedlings go into the garden.

Like the containers that will hold the seeds, the medium in which they are to be planted should also be sterile, to minimize the risk of pathogens. The medium should be porous and light-textured, so delicate roots can easily find spaces to grow, and so excess water can drain off. At the same time, the medium must be able to hold enough moisture to allow seeds to absorb what they need in order to germinate.

The seed-starting mixture may or may not contain soil. Soilless mixes are generally sterile, but they contain no nutrients to feed the tiny plants after germination occurs; you, the gardener, will have to supply their needs. Soil contains nutrients that will nourish the young plants, but it also contains microorganisms, some of which can be harmful to delicate seedlings. If you add soil to the planting medium, use sterilized, packaged potting soil, or pasteurize garden soil by pouring boiling water over it and sealing the hot soil in a plastic bag until it cools.

Besides soil, the ingredients most often used in germination media are peat moss, perlite, vermiculite, finely milled sphagnum moss, and sharp builder's sand.

You can blend your own seed-starting medium or buy a packaged mix at a local garden center. It comes down to a decision between convenience and control. Many of the commercial mixes contain fertilizers, which eliminate the need for you to fertilize the seedlings yourself before you transplant them to the garden. But if the fertilizers are too strong they will overstimulate the seedlings, causing them to grow too rapidly and thus weakening them. Such seedlings will have a difficult time adjusting to conditions in the garden, and may never perform as well as they should.

The goal is to produce stocky, compact seedlings that will quickly make the transition to the garden after transplanting. If you use a soilless medium and fertilize the seedlings yourself, start with a liquid fertilizer diluted to one-quarter the recommended strength, and gradually increase to a half-strength formula as the seedlings grow.

To start seeds, fill the containers with medium to about a half-inch from the top. The medium should be moist but not soggy. If you are using peat pots, soak them in water before filling them.

Scatter the seeds evenly over the surface of the medium, or place one or two seeds in each compartment of a cell pack. It is important not to sow seeds too thickly, or you will wind up with crowds of tiny seedlings that will be very difficult to thin without damaging the fragile roots. Press the seeds gently into the medium, so they are just barely covered. As an added disease–preventive, you can sift a thin layer of milled sphagnum moss on top of the medium.

Unless the medium is very moist, set the container in a pan of room-temperature water until the surface of the medium feels wet to the touch. Then remove the container and let it drain. If you prefer, mist the medium to dampen it instead—either method will wet the medium without disturbing the seeds. Keep the medium evenly moist, but not soggy; touch the soil with your finger every day to see if it feels damp.

Label the containers as soon as you plant the seeds, so you won't forget what's planted where.

Many seeds germinate best in warm soil. You can supply bottom heat by purchasing electric heating mats made especially for this purpose. Don't use a heating pad—it may get too hot and it will not be waterproof.

Cover the containers with plastic to maintain high humidity. If using a plastic bag, place sticks in the corners of the container to hold the bag away from the soil. Open the cover for a while each day to let in fresh air.

When the seedlings pop through the soil surface, give them as much light as you can. Bright, unobstructed south and east windows are both good places for seedlings. If you live in a warm climate, though, a south-facing window may get too hot, and an eastern exposure would be a better choice. If the windowsills are too narrow to hold the containers, push a table right up against the sills to hold the pots or flats. If you grow your seedlings in a window, turn the containers every day so the stems grow straight. Remove the plastic covers, too, or the sun will cook your seedlings. Set the containers on trays of pebbles filled with water to increase humidity (the bottoms of the containers should not sit in the water).

Reflecting additional light onto windowsill seedlings is helpful. White-painted surfaces are highly reflective. You can also line the windowsill with aluminum foil, and place a foil reflector between the plants and the room.

If you do not have suitable windows for raising seedlings, or you don't want to clutter up the windowsills with plants, set up a light garden for your plant nursery. Ordinary fluorescent fixtures are an excellent light source for plants. Use daylight or wide-spectrum tubes for the best results. Many gardeners set up a light garden in the basement.

The lights should be about four inches above the tops of the plants when they are small. When the plants get to be about six inches tall, their tops should be six to ten inches below the lights. Suspending the light fixtures on chains makes it easy to adjust their height. Or you can place the seedling containers on stacks of books or bricks, removing one book at a time as the plants grow. Have the lights on fourteen to sixteen hours a day.

Check daily to see if the plants need water. Feed the seedlings once or twice a week with mild liquid fertilizer, that is, fertilizer diluted to one-half or one-quarter of the recommended strength. Most seedlings will be ready to go into the garden six to eight weeks after planting, if weather conditions are suitable.

Hardening-Off

Before seedlings started indoors can go out to the garden they must be gradually acclimated to the harsher conditions of the outdoor garden, a process known as "hardening-off." Hardening-off is important, because seedlings damaged by cold (or heat, in the case of seedlings started indoors in summer) will at best suffer growth setbacks; they may even be killed, and all your hard work will have gone to waste.

To harden-off seedlings place them outdoors in a sheltered spot for a couple of hours the first day, then bring them back indoors. Each succeeding day, leave the plants outdoors for two to three hours longer than the day before. After seven to ten days, let the seedlings stay outdoors overnight. By this time the seedlings should be tough enough to survive outdoors. If bad weather strikes during the hardening-off period, leave the seedlings indoors or under cover, and extend the process for several more days.

Order nursery stock for early spring planting. If weather permits, begin to prune and shape trees and shrubs, except for spring bloomers.

1-3

Order nursery stock for early spring planting. If weather permits, begin to prune and shape trees and shrubs, except for spring bloomers. When temperature goes above 40 degrees F, check for overwintering pests and apply dormant oil sprays.

4

Order nursery stock for early spring planting. Continue dormant pruning. When temperature goes above 40 degrees F, check for overwintering pests and apply dormant oil sprays. Check tree guards. Check climbers to be sure they are still fastened to their supports.

5

Continue pruning; do not prune spring bloomers except to remove weak and damaged branches. During dry spells, pull aside mulch and water fall-planted trees and shrubs, and shallow-rooters such as azaleas. Check tree guards. Check supports on young trees and climbers; reset if heaved by frost. Apply dormant oil sprays on mild days.

6

Plant bare-root stock (see page 15). Continue pruning; do not prune spring bloomers except to remove weak and damaged branches. During dry spells, water fall-planted trees and shrubs, and shallow rooters such as azaleas. Check tree guards. Check supports on climbers and young trees; reset if heaved by frost.

7

Plant bare-root stock while still dormant. Plant balled-and-burlapped and container-grown stock. Continue pruning dormant trees and shrubs. Fertilize established trees, shrubs, vines, evergreens. Fertilize newly planted stock. Remove winter mulches. Layer shrubs as soon as soil can be worked.

8

Finish planting bare-root stock while still dormant. Plant balled-and-burlapped and container-grown stock. Fertilize established trees, shrubs, and vines, and newly planted stock; wait one to two months after planting to fertilize citrus. Water deeply during dry weather. Remove winter mulches. Layer shrubs.

9

Plant balled-and-burlapped and container-grown stock. Fertilize established and newly planted trees, shrubs and vines; wait one to two months after planting to fertilize citrus. Water deeply during dry weather. Layer shrubs.

10-11

	Roses	Lawns & Ground Covers
1-3	Order shrub roses for spring planting.	Use sand or ashes on icy walks and driveways—salt damages lawns and other plants. Avoid walking on frozen grass with no snow cover.
4	Order roses for early spring planting.	See Zone 3
5	Order roses for early spring planting. Check supports for climbers; replace any detached canes.	Use sand or ashes on icy walks and driveways—salt damages lawns and other plants. Avoid walking on frozen grass with no snow cover. Get lawn mower ready for spring: clean, sharpen blade.
6	Order roses for early spring planting. Check supports for climbers; replace any detached canes. Prune bush roses before new growth begins.	See Zone 5
7	Order roses for early spring planting if you have not already done so. Check supports for climbers; replace any detached canes. Prune bush roses before new growth begins.	Use sand or ashes on icy walks and driveways—salt damages lawns and other plants. Get lawn mower ready for spring: clean, sharpen blade. Cut back ornamental grasses before new growth begins.
8	Plant bare-root roses while still dormant. Fertilize established plants when new growth appears. Prune bush roses before new growth begins.	Lightly fertilize lawns and ground covers as they begin to grow. Aerate lawn; de-thatch if necessary. Trim messy-looking ground covers. Cut back ornamental grasses if not done last month.
9	Fertilize established roses when new growth begins. Water deeply once a week during dry spells.	Lightly fertilize lawns and ground covers as they begin to grow, if not done last month. Aerate lawn; de-thatch if necessary. Trim messy-looking ground covers. Water lawns if weather is dry.
10-11	See Zone 9	Lightly fertilize lawns and ground covers as they begin to grow, if not done last month. Aerate lawn; de-thatch if necessary. Trim shaggy ground covers if not done last month. Water lawns if weather is dry.

Perennials

Order perennials for spring planting. Check mulches in beds and borders. Check for frost heaving; replace or cover any exposed roots. Finish drawing or revising plans for beds and borders.

Order perennials for spring planting. Sow seeds indoors for transplanting out in spring. Check mulches in beds and borders. Check for frost heaving; replace or cover any exposed roots. Finish drawing or revising plans for beds and borders.

See Zone 4

Order perennials for spring planting. Sow seeds indoors for transplanting out in spring. Check for slug damage to tender crowns; if present, sprinkle coarse sand or wood ashes around base of plants. Check mulches in beds and borders. Check for frost heaving; replace or cover any exposed roots. Finish drawing or revising plans for beds and borders.

Finish ordering plants. Sow perennials indoors or in cold frame. If weather is mild, begin removing winter mulches. Weed and clean up beds and borders. If weather is still cold, check for frost heaving; replace or cover any exposed roots.

Sow perennials indoors or in cold frame. Begin removing winter mulches. Weed and clean up beds and borders. Fertilize established plants when they begin to grow. Dig and divide summer and autumn bloomers.

Plant spring bloomers. Fertilize established plants when they begin to grow. Dig and divide summer and autumn bloomers. Weed and clean up beds and borders.

See Zone 9

1-3

Check mulches on bulb beds; replace if necessary.

Order seeds if not done last month. Sow slow-growing annuals indoors. Care for indoor plants started from cuttings from last summer's garden.

4

Check mulches on bulb beds; replace if necessary. Check summer bulbs stored indoors; discard any with mold, rot, or soft spots; mist if starting to dry out.

Sow slow-growing annuals indoors. Cut back geraniums stored indoors over winter. Take cuttings of geraniums, wax begonias, coleus to start new plants for this year's garden. Pinch back plants started indoors last month.

5

Check mulches on bulb beds; replace if necessary. Check summer bulbs stored indoors; discard any with mold, rot, or soft spots; mist if drying out. Divide clumps of dahlia roots.

See Zone 4

6

Start tuberous begonias indoors in bright light (no direct sun). Check summer bulbs stored indoors. Divide clumps of dahlia roots. Fertilize early spring bulbs as shoots appear. Sprinkle wood ashes around spring bulbs if slugs are a problem.

See Zone 4

7

See Zone 6

Sow hardy annuals outdoors; sow sweet peas in rich soil. Sow summer bloomers indoors. Cut back geraniums stored indoors over winter. Take cuttings of geraniums, wax begonias, coleus to start new plants for this year's garden. Pinch back plants started indoors last month.

8

Start tuberous begonias, caladiums, dahlias indoors in bright light to plant out next month. Fertilize spring bulbs as shoots appear. Sprinkle wood ashes around spring bulbs if slugs are a problem.

Direct-sow or transplant out hardy annuals; sow sweet peas; set out pansies. Sow tender summer annuals indoors to plant out after last frost. Take cuttings of geraniums, wax begonias, coleus to start new plants for this year's garden. Pinch back plants started indoors last month.

9

See Zone 8

Plant out hardy annuals; sow sweet peas; set out pansies. Late in month begin to harden-off tender annuals in cold frame. Pinch back plants growing indoors or in cold frame. Deadhead winter annuals; remove worn-out plants.

10-11

Start planting summer bulbs outdoors; plant gladiolus in successions two weeks apart. Fertilize spring bulbs as shoots appear; sprinkle wood ashes if slugs are a problem.

See Zone 9

Container Gardens	Vegetables & Herbs	
Finish cleaning pots and containers. Disinfect clay pots by soaking in bleach solution. Check tender container plants moved indoors for winter.	Notice where snow melts first in garden; mark these spots for planting early crops. Clean lights used for starting seeds indoors.	*1-3*
See Zone 3	Notice where snow melts first in garden; mark these spots for planting early crops. Sow earliest crops indoors.	*4*
Finish cleaning pots and containers. Disinfect clay pots by soaking in bleach solution. Inventory supplies; stock up for spring planting. Check container plants moved indoors for winter.	Notice where snow melts first in garden; mark these spots for planting early crops. Sow earliest crops indoors; late in month sow peppers and eggplant.	*5*
Finish cleaning pots and containers. Disinfect clay pots by soaking in bleach solution. Inventory supplies; stock up for spring planting. Check container plants moved indoors for winter.	Sow in cold frame salad greens, beets, onions, parsley, cabbage family. Start seed potatoes indoors. Fertilize or top-dress asparagus with compost if not done last fall.	*6*
Finish cleaning pots and containers. Disinfect clay pots by soaking in bleach solution. Inventory and restock supplies if not done last month. Check container plants moved indoors for winter.	Direct-sow early peas and spinach; protect with hot caps, etc. Sow in cold frame salad greens, beets, onions, parsley, cabbage family. Start seed potatoes. Fertilize or top-dress asparagus with compost if not done last fall. Till in cover crops when soil permits.	*7*
Finish cleaning pots and containers. Disinfect clay pots by soaking in bleach solution. Inventory and restock supplies if not done last month. Check container plants moved indoors for winter. Prune shrubs in containers while dormant.	Direct-sow cold-tolerant crops. In southern areas, set out early cabbage family transplants; cover during hard freezes. Plant asparagus roots. Sow summer vegetables and tender herbs indoors or in cold frame. Open cold frame to ventilate when temperature exceeds 40 degrees F. Prepare soil for planting later crops.	*8*
Plant hardy annuals in containers; water as needed. Prune container shrubs while dormant.	Direct-sow cold-tolerant vegetables and herbs. Set out transplants of spring crops. Sow warm-season vegetables and herbs indoors or in cold frame. Fertilize vegetable seedlings with mild liquid fertilizer. Ventilate cold frame on mild days. Prepare soil for planting later crops.	*9*
See Zone 9	Direct-sow and set out transplants of cold-tolerant vegetables and herbs. Sow warm-season crops indoors or in cold frame. Fertilize vegetable seedlings with mild liquid fertilizer. Open cold frame to ventilate when temperature exceeds 40 degrees F. Prepare soil for planting later crops.	*10-11*

1-3

Check mouse guards and tree wraps. When weather permits, prune trees, berries, brambles, and grapes. On mild days check for overwintering pests and apply dormant oil sprays.

4

Order strawberries for spring planting. Prune trees, berries, brambles, and grapes. Check mouse guards and tree wraps. On mild days check for overwintering pests and apply dormant oil sprays.

5

See Zone 4

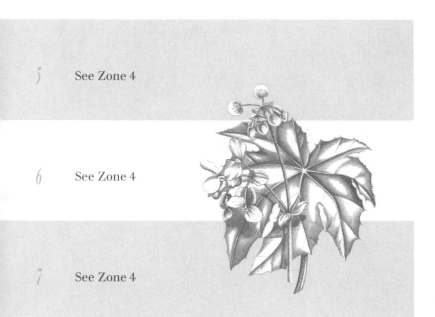

6

See Zone 4

7

See Zone 4

8

Plant strawberries and bare-root nursery stock. Finish pruning while plants are still dormant. Fertilize established berries and fruit trees if not done last month.

9

See Zone 8

10-11

Plant strawberries and bare-root nursery stock. Fertilize established citrus and tropical fruits.

Testing for Germination

If you have saved leftover seeds for a year or two, it is wise to test them for viability before planting in the garden. To test for germination, take ten seeds and lay them on a moist paper towel. Roll up the towel and place it inside a plastic bag. Fasten the top of the bag with a twist-tie. Open the bag every couple of days to check that the towel is still moist. After seven days, unroll it and check for germination. If only a few of the seeds have sprouted, roll up the towel and put it back in the bag for another few days. If, after ten days, only one or two seeds have germinated, throw out the stored seeds and buy new ones. If seven or more seeds have sprouted, the seeds are still quite viable.

A shortcut way to test viability is to drop a handful of seeds into a cup of room-temperature water. Any seeds that float are not viable. Good seeds will usually sink to the bottom.

Seed-Starting Mix

A classic recipe for a seed-starting medium is one developed at Cornell University years ago and still widely used today. It is quite simple: mix equal parts of peat moss, perlite, and vermiculite.

March

Planting Trees, Shrubs, and Roses

Spring planting of bare-root trees, shrubs, and roses begins as soon as it is possible to dig holes for them. Holes may even be dug in advance where the outdoor growing season is short. For many gardeners, March is the time to plant nursery stock. Here are some guidelines for doing it properly.

Many perennial plants are sold in bare-root form, by mail-order nurseries and local retailers. Bare-root plants are shipped and planted while they are dormant. You will find deciduous trees and shrubs, roses, small evergreens, some herbaceous perennials, and asparagus sold bare-root.

When you buy bare-root stock, the roots should be wrapped in damp sphagnum moss, excelsior, or other packing material to keep them moist and cushion them during shipping. Roots and packing material are in turn packaged in containers of cardboard, heavy waxed paper, or plastic.

Check bare-root stock carefully before planting. The canes or branches should be firm and healthy-looking. There should be no new shoots longer than an inch or so (the plants are supposed to be dormant). If buying locally, do not buy bare-root stock before you are ready to plant it and weather conditions are suitable.

As soon as you get the plants home, or the shipping service delivers them, open the packages and set the plants in buckets of water deep enough to cover the roots. Let them soak for several hours or overnight; then get the plants into the ground. If you cannot plant within a day or two of receiving the plants, set them on an angle in a shallow trench and cover the roots loosely with soil (this procedure is called heeling-in).

Dig a generous-sized hole for each plant, about a foot wider than the spread of the roots. When in doubt, make the hole too large instead of too small. Make the hole deep enough so that you can position the plant at the same depth at which it had been growing in the nursery. Look for a soil line on the stem and plant so the soil surface will match the line. If you cannot see a soil line, look for the point at which the roots join the stem; for most plants this point should be one to two inches underground after planting. When the hole is ready, toss a shovelful of compost into the bottom and mix it into the soil. Make a mound of soil in the bottom of the hole.

Remove the plant from its bucket of water, and cut off any damaged parts of roots. Mix some mud into the bucket of water and dip the roots into this slurry to coat them (it will help keep them moist after planting). Set the plant on the soil mound in the bottom of the hole, check the depth, and carefully spread the roots out and down over the sides of the mound.

Fill the hole halfway with soil, then water to settle the soil around the roots. Fill the hole the rest of the way, water again, and rock the plant gently back and forth to make sure the roots make good contact with the soil.

Planting times for balled-and-burlapped and container-grown trees and shrubs are less critical than for bare-root stock. Both can go into the ground anytime during the growing season, although spring and fall, when the weather is mild and least stressful for plants, are the best times.

It is best to plant balled-and-burlapped plants as soon as you get them home from the nursery. But if you cannot plant right away, set the plant in a shady spot, make sure the soil ball is moist, and cover the ball with loose mulch.

Dig the planting hole one and a half to two feet deeper and wider than the root ball, and mix some compost into the bottom of the hole. Set the plant into the hole. If the wrapping around the soil ball is tied with ropes, cut them off. If the wrapping is real burlap you can leave it in place to decay naturally in the soil. Just roll back the edges and make sure they are underground when the hole is filled in. If the wrapping is an imitation burlap that is actually plastic, you will have to remove it.

Work carefully to keep the soil ball intact. The top of the soil ball should be even with the soil level when the plant is in the hole. Fill in around the root ball with soil, firming it in place but not packing it too tightly. Fill the hole halfway with soil, water to settle it, fill the hole the rest of the way, and water again.

Container-grown plants are handled much the same way. If the plant does not slide easily out of its container, lay the container carefully on its side and roll it on the ground, pressing to loosen the soil from the sides of the container. If roots are growing through the drainage holes in the bottom of the pot, clip them off so they do not hold the plant to the container.

No matter what form a tree or shrub is in when you plant it—bare-root, balled-and-burlapped, or container-grown—some roots are bound to be lost during transplanting. It is necessary to prune some of the topgrowth to put less of a strain on the remaining roots while they are getting established in the soil. Container-grown plants usually need less pruning than the other two types of stock—just cut off weak and damaged branches and prune lightly to shape the plant. For bare-root and balled-

and-burlapped stock, cut back the topgrowth by up to one-third at planting time.

Pay particular attention to the branch structure when planting fruit trees. Remove any branches that emerge from the main trunk at an angle of less than 45 degrees. The branches you leave on a young fruit tree at this stage of its development become the basic framework, or scaffold, that will support the weight of the fruit in subsequent years. Branches meeting the trunk at an angle greater than 45 degrees will be stronger and better able to bear the load than sharply angled branches.

If your new tree has a trunk larger than an inch in diameter, it is a good idea to stake it after planting. Drive a long wooden stake—about eight feet—into the ground next to the trunk. If you live in a particularly windy area, drive in a second stake on the opposite side of the trunk from the first one. Attach the tree to the stake with a piece of heavy-gauge wire threaded through a piece of old garden hose where it touches the trunk, or use strips of cloth or soft rope. Fasten the tie securely, but not so tightly that it cuts into the tree.

Another helpful practice is to wrap the tender-barked trunks of young trees with tree-wrap paper to prevent sunscald, cut down on moisture loss, and keep borers from tunneling into the wood. Start at the point where the lowest branch meets the trunk, and wrap downward in neat, overlapping spirals, all the way to the base of the trunk. Leave the tree wrap in place for up to two years.

Like all new transplants, newly planted trees and shrubs will establish themselves most readily in soil that is evenly moist. In hot, dry weather when you receive less than an inch of rain every week or so, water new trees and shrubs deeply twice a week. Deep watering is important; shallow surface watering encourages plants to send lots of feeder roots into the upper levels of the soil, making your trees and shrubs less able to tolerate drought and hot sun. Deep watering will encourage plants to send roots downward into the soil, where they will be less prone to damage during dry spells. There is some debate in horticultural circles about how deep the soil really needs to be moistened, but a depth of two feet would seem to be a minimum, at least for relatively shallow-rooted plants.

It is a good idea to mulch newly planted trees and shrubs during their first year in the garden. Lay down a three- to four-inch layer of shredded leaves, compost, salt hay, wood chips, or other loose, organic mulch to help conserve soil moisture, moderate the soil temperature, and keep down weeds. If you are planting in early spring, wait for the soil to warm up before spreading the mulch. If planting in fall, you can lay the mulch right away. In late fall, pull the mulch about eight inches away from the trunks of trees, to discourage mice from turning it into a cozy winter retreat where they can nibble at the tender bark whenever they like. You may want to install mouse guards for winter (see page 49).

Fertilize established trees and shrubs before growth begins.

Prune trees if wood is no longer frozen. Fertilize established trees and shrubs before growth starts. Check for overwintering pests and if necessary, apply dormant oil sprays when temperature is above 40 degrees F.

Plant bare-root stock when soil permits. Prune trees if wood is no longer frozen; prune damaged wood from hedges and shrubs. Fertilize established trees and shrubs. Remove winter protection: mulches, wraps, screens, and shelters. Check for overwintering pests and, if necessary, apply dormant oil sprays when temperature goes above 40 degrees F.

Plant bare-root stock when soil permits. Prune damaged wood from trees, shrubs, and hedges, except for spring bloomers. Fertilize evergreens and flowering shrubs and trees. Remove winter protection: mulches, wraps, screens, and shelters. Check for pests and, if necessary, apply dormant oil sprays before new growth begins. Layer shrubs as soon as soil is workable.

Plant bare-root stock. Prune damaged wood from trees, shrubs, and hedges, except for spring bloomers. Fertilize evergreens and flowering shrubs and trees. Top-dress trees and shrubs with compost. Layer shrubs as soon as soil is workable.

Continue planting trees, shrubs, and vines; make sure bare-root stock gets into the ground while still dormant. Finish pruning winter damage. Shear hedges if needed. Trim topiaries and espaliered trees. Fertilize new and established trees, shrubs, and vines if not done last month. Watch for pests.

Continue planting if weather is still cool enough; plant subtropical plants when all danger of frost is past. Prune spring bloomers as they finish flowering. Finish fertilizing new and established trees, shrubs, and vines.

Plant tropical and subtropical trees, shrubs, and vines. Prune spring bloomers as they finish flowering. Finish fertilizing new and established trees, shrubs, and vines.

1-3

If weather permits, prune shrub roses while still dormant, if not done last fall. Begin to gradually remove winter protection when ground starts to thaw.

4

See Zone 3

5

Prune winter-damaged growth. Begin to gradually remove winter protection as ground thaws. Fertilize established roses.

Trim ground covers that need it. Cut back ornamental grasses before they begin to grow. Fertilize ground covers. Fertilize lawn—lightly if you fertilized last fall. Test soil pH in lawn if you have not done so in several years.

6

Plant bare-root roses as soon as soil is workable. Prune winter-damaged growth. Remove winter mulches. Fertilize established roses.

See Zone 5

7

Plant bare-root roses; cut back stems to six inches. Prune roses: remove weak, dead, damaged shoots; cut back strong shoots by half. Fertilize established roses. Begin to watch for pests and signs of disease

Start new lawns from seed or sod. Begin mowing lawn when grass is three inches high. Trim ground covers that need it. Cut back ornamental grasses before they begin to grow. Fertilize ground covers. Fertilize lawn—lightly if you fertilized last fall. De-thatch, if necessary, and aerate lawn. Test soil pH in lawn if you have not done so in several years.

8

Continue planting. Complete pruning. Fertilize roses monthly. Water after fertilizing, and when necessary because of dry weather. Watch for pests and signs of disease.

Overseed thin or bare spots in lawn. Begin mowing when grass is three inches high. Fertilize ground covers if not done last month. Water lawns when needed during dry weather. Test soil pH in lawn if you have not done so in several years.

9

Continue to fertilize established roses; wait to fertilize new plants until after the first flush of bloom. Water weekly during dry weather. Watch for pests and signs of disease.

Start new lawns from seed or sod; overseed thin or bare spots. Begin mowing lawn when grass is three inches high. Water lawns when needed during dry weather. Test soil pH in lawn if you have not done so in several years.

10-11

See Zone 9

See Zone 9

	Perennials	Bulbs
1-3	Sow perennials indoors to plant out later in spring.	Check mulches on bulb beds; replace if necessary.
4	Sow perennials indoors to plant out later in spring. Gradually remove winter mulch from beds and borders.	Gradually remove mulch when shoots of early bulbs begin to grow. Fertilize as growth gets under way. Check begonia tubers stored indoors; plant in pots or flats when they start to sprout.
5	Finish sowing perennials indoors to plant out later. Gradually remove winter mulch from beds and borders. Fertilize established perennials as they begin to grow.	See Zone 4
6	Fertilize established perennials as they begin to grow. Remove remaining winter mulches from beds and borders; clean up any debris. While plants are young, note which ones will need division later in season.	Gradually remove winter mulch when shoots of early bulbs begin to grow. Fertilize as growth gets under way. Plant summer bulbs (tuberous begonia, dahlia, caladium) in flats or pots indoors to transplant out in May.
7	See Zone 6	Fertilize bulbs as growth gets under way. Plant summer bulbs (tuberous begonia, dahlia, caladium) in flats or pots indoors to transplant out in May.
8	Continue planting and transplanting perennials. Dig and divide crowded summer and fall bloomers. Lightly fertilize established plants as they begin to grow. Water as necessary. Deadhead faded flowers. Put stakes in place for tall growers that will need them. Mulch new plants. Edge and weed beds and borders. Watch for pests and signs of disease.	Order summer blooming bulbs to plant outdoors after last frost. Fertilize spring bulbs as they finish blooming. Deadhead faded flowers but leave foliage to mature. Make notes on areas where you want more bulbs and plan now to order for fall planting.
9	Lightly fertilize established plants as they begin to grow. Water as necessary. Deadhead faded flowers. Make sure stakes are in place for tall growers that will need them. Edge and weed beds and borders. Watch for pests and signs of disease.	Plant out summer bulbs when frost danger is past. Fertilize spring bulbs when they finish blooming. Deadhead faded flowers but leave foliage to mature. Make notes on areas where you want more bulbs and plan now to order for fall planting.
10-11	See Zone 9	Plant summer bulbs outdoors. Fertilize spring bulbs when they finish blooming. Deadhead faded flowers but leave foliage to mature. Make notes on areas where you want more bulbs and plan now to order for fall planting.

Annuals

Sow slow-growing annuals indoors. Care for indoor plants started from cuttings from last summer's garden. Take cuttings of geraniums, wax begonias, coleus to start new plants for this year's garden. Cut back geraniums kept indoors over winter, to rejuvenate them and start new growth. Pinch back plants started indoors last month.

Sow slow-growing annuals indoors if not already done. Direct-sow hardy annuals. Care for indoor plants started from cuttings last fall. Take cuttings of geraniums, wax begonias, coleus to start new plants for this year's garden. Cut back geraniums kept indoors over winter, to rejuvenate them and start new growth. Pinch back seedlings started indoors last month.

Sow slow-growing annuals indoors if not already done. Direct-sow hardy annuals; sow sweet peas as soon as soil is workable. Care for indoor plants started from cuttings last fall. Take cuttings of geraniums, wax begonias, coleus to start new plants for this year's garden. Cut back geraniums kept indoors over winter, to rejuvenate them and start new growth. Pinch back seedlings started indoors last month.

Direct-sow hardy annuals; sow sweet peas as soon as soil is workable. Sow tender annuals indoors to plant out when weather warms. Plant out pansies when weather settles; feed, water, and deadhead often. Prepare garden soil for later planting. Pinch back seedlings growing indoors.

Direct-sow hardy annuals and sweet peas. Sow tender annuals indoors to plant out after frost danger is past. Plant out pansies; feed, water, and deadhead often. Prepare garden soil for later planting. Pinch back seedlings growing indoors.

Continue planting hardy annuals outdoors. Continue sowing tender annuals indoors. Thin seedlings. Deadhead, weed, and water as needed; fertilize pansies. Edge beds and borders.

Direct-sow or transplant out tender annuals when frost danger is past. Overplant bulb beds with annuals to hide bulb foliage. Deadhead winter annuals to keep them blooming. Thin seedlings. Deadhead, weed, and water as needed. Edge beds and borders.

Direct-sow or transplant out tender annuals. Overplant bulb beds with annuals to hide bulb foliage. Deadhead winter annuals to keep them blooming. Thin seedlings. Feed winter annuals and new transplants with water-soluble fertilizer. Deadhead, weed, and water as needed. Edge beds and borders.

	Container Gardens	Vegetables & Herbs
1–3	Check tender container plants moved indoors for winter. Inventory supplies; stock up for spring planting.	Note where snow melts first in garden and mark these spots for planting early crops. Sow cabbage family indoors. In zone 3, sow summer crops indoors late this month.
4	See Zone 3	Direct-sow earliest crops when soil begins to warm. Sow summer crops indoors late this month; use individual peat pots for squash. Care for seedlings growing indoors. Clean up garden areas for later planting. Test soil if not done recently.
5	Check tender container plants moved indoors for winter. Inventory and restock supplies if not done last month. Prune shrubs in containers while dormant.	Dig root crops left in garden from last fall. Prepare soil and direct-sow earliest crops as soon as soil is workable. Begin to harden-off brassica seedlings: plant out when soil is workable. Care for indoor seedlings; adjust height of lights, turn windowsill seedlings daily, water, fertilize. Fertilize asparagus. Clean up garden and prepare soil for planting later crops.
6	See Zone 5	Sow summer vegetables and tender herbs indoors—adjust height of lights, turn windowsill seedlings daily, water, fertilize. Cover outdoor seedlings if you expect a heavy frost. Dig in cover crops. Set up supports for peas.
7	Begin setting up for spring planting; move large containers outdoors and fill with potting mix. Plant hardy annuals and cold-tolerant vegetables when danger of heavy frost is past.	Dig root crops left in garden from last fall. Direct-sow and transplant out spring crops. Sow summer vegetables and tender herbs indoors. Cover outdoor plants if you expect a heavy frost. Clean up garden and prepare soil for planting later crops; dig in cover crops. Fertilize asparagus. Set up supports for peas. Care for indoor seedlings: adjust height of lights, turn windowsill seedlings daily, water, fertilize.
8	Begin spring planting. Move large containers outdoors and fill with potting mix. Plant hardy annuals and cold-tolerant vegetables.	Direct-sow and transplant out spring crops. Sow summer vegetables and tender herbs in cold frame (open on warm days). Plant out when frost danger is past. Prune perennial herbs. Clean up garden. Prepare soil for planting later crops. Dig in cover crops. Fertilize asparagus. Set up supports for peas. Watch for pests. Adjust height of lights, turn windowsill seedlings daily, water and fertilize indoor seedlings.
9	Plant tender annuals when frost danger is past; continue to plant cold-tolerant vegetables. Water container plants as needed; fertilize with water-soluble fertilizer. Move tender container plants stored indoors over winter back outdoors when frost danger is past.	Direct-sow and transplant out spring crops. Sow or transplant summer vegetables and tender herbs when frost danger is past. Prune perennial herbs. Fertilize asparagus. Set up supports for peas. Watch for pests. Open cold frame on warm days. Thin seedlings.
10–11	Plant tender annuals, summer vegetables, and herbs in containers. Water container plants as needed; fertilize with water-soluble fertilizer. When frost danger is past, move back outdoors any tropical container plants brought indoors for winter.	Direct-sow and transplant out spring crops. Sow or transplant summer vegetables and tender herbs when weather is warm enough. Set up supports for peas and beans. Watch for pests. Open cold frame on warm days. Thin seedlings.

Fruit

Prune trees and berries before new growth begins, when wood is not frozen. Plant bare-root stock as soon as soil can be worked. Clean up any dropped fruit and leaves.

Prune trees and berries before new growth begins, when wood is not frozen, while plants are still dormant. Plant bare-root stock as soon as soil can be worked. Clean up any dropped fruit and leaves.

Plant bare-root stock as soon as soil can be worked. Plant strawberries. Finish pruning while plants are still dormant. Fertilize berries and grapes.

Plant bare-root stock as soon as soil can be worked. Plant strawberries. Prune and thin brambles if not done last fall; reapply mulch. Finish pruning while plants are still dormant. Fertilize fruit trees. Gradually remove mulch from established strawberries; remove or replace plants heaved by frost.

Finish planting bare-root stock while still dormant. Plant strawberries. Fertilize trees, bushes, brambles, and grapevines. Remove mulch from established strawberries; remove or replace any plants heaved by frost.

Plant balled-and-burlapped and container-grown stock. Fertilize bushes, brambles, and grapevines. Watch out for fire blight symptoms.

Plant balled-and-burlapped and container-grown stock; plant citrus when frost danger is past. Deeply water established citrus when it blooms. Watch out for fire blight and pests.

Plant balled-and-burlapped and container-grown stock; plant citrus when weather is warm enough. Deeply water established citrus when it blooms. Watch out for pests and disease symptoms.

How to Buy Healthy Plants

When confronted with the sea of plants at local garden centers, it can be difficult to pick out the best specimens to take home for your garden. Here are some tips on recognizing a healthy plant.

First, biggest is not usually best. Do not buy plants that look top-heavy or too big for their containers. Smaller plants transplant more easily and make the transition to the garden more quickly.

Look for stocky plants with firm stems and, unless they are colored-leaved varieties, foliage with good green color.

Look for plants with leaves spaced closely on stems; lanky plants with widely spaced leaves probably have not been getting enough light.

Look for plants with healthy new growth around the top and the tips of branching stems.

Check to see that the soil in the containers is moist—neither dry nor soggy. If plants are limp from water stress, don't buy them.

Look closely for signs of disease: don't buy plants with soft, mushy, or discolored spots on leaves; with discolored leaf veins or brown, dry leaves or leaf edges; or with fuzzy growth on stems or leaves.

Check for insects; examine the undersides of leaves, leaf axils (where leaves join stem), and new growth. If you see little specks, recognizable bugs, fine webbing, or cottony patches, do not buy the plant.

Look for plants that appear vigorous and healthy and that are kept in conditions like those they will need in the garden—shade plants kept out of direct sun, for example.

April

Planting Outdoors

Spring planting of nonwoody plants begins as the weather settles and the soil thaws and warms. Warm-climate gardeners begin planting before April, but for gardeners farther north, planting gets under way in earnest in April and May.

When the garden soil has been prepared, and weather conditions are congenial, spring planting can begin. Cold-hardy vegetables, herbs, and flowers can go into the ground several weeks before the last frost occurs. Tender plants, which would be damaged by frost, must wait until all danger of frost is past. Your local USDA County Extension office can tell you the average date of the last spring frost in your area. See also the information on phenology on page viii for guidance on determining safe planting times.

Whether you are planting hardy (cool-season) or tender (warm-season) seeds or plants, be sure the soil is properly prepared (see page x for information). Seeds and young seedlings grow most readily in a light, loose, fine-textured soil that is crumbly and well-supplied with nutrients.

The best day to plant or transplant is one that is overcast but not windy, when temperatures are moderate. If you want to plant on a sunny day, particularly in a warm climate or during the summer, do the planting in the morning, when the sun will not be as hot and stressful for the young plants as it will be closer to noon. Do not plant when heavy rain is expected, or when the ground is still wet from earlier rains. If a late cold snap has made the weather harsher than is normal for the time of year, wait an extra week or two before setting out or seeding tender plants.

If you will be planting seedlings you raised indoors or bought from a garden center where they were kept in a greenhouse, be sure they are hardened-off before planting (see page 9).

Late in the afternoon of the day before you expect to transplant, water the seedlings and the garden area where you will plant them.

Make the necessary drills or furrows if you are sowing seeds, or holes for plants. Space planting holes at the distance the plants will need when they reach their mature size. Holes should be large enough to allow the plant to sit at the same depth at which it was growing in the container. Exceptions must be made to this rule if you are planting in warm climates where summer weather will be quite hot, or transplanting seedlings that are spindly and elongated from lack of light. In both these sit-

uations it is usually best to position the plants deeper than they were previously growing.

Remove the plant carefully from its container. If the plant does not slide out easily, tap the bottom and sides of the pot with the handle of a trowel to loosen the soil. Turn the pot over with one hand, supporting the top of the root ball at the base of the stem with your other hand. Slip the plant out of the pot, support the root ball underneath, and set the plant in the hole. If you are working with young seedlings, hold the plant gently by two upper leaves (*not* the stem) and provide support under the root ball with a spoon or your finger when transferring the plant from pot to garden.

Fill the hole with soil, firming it around the plant but not packing it hard. Water well, to settle the soil around the roots, fill the hole again, and water again. If you live where dry weather is likely, make a saucerlike depression in the soil around the base of the plant to capture and hold water around the roots.

If you are transplanting seedlings in peat pots, tear the sides of each pot to make it easy for roots to grow out into the garden soil. Be sure the rim of the pot is completely buried after planting or it may act as a wick and draw the moisture from the walls of the pot in dry weather.

Thinning

Seedlings growing from seeds sown directly outdoors in the garden, or in undivided flats indoors, will almost certainly need thinning. Unless you have a very steady hand and great patience when sowing, it is nearly impossible to drop seeds—especially tiny ones—at the ideal spacing distance.

It can be tempting to avoid thinning a stand of seedlings—they must be moved with great care, it can be difficult to find extra space for them, and it seems somehow cruel to uproot the tiny things. But thin you must. Crowded plants will never grow well; they remain smaller and produce fewer, poorer flowers or less of a crop because they are competing with one another for moisture, nutrients, and growing space. Allowing enough space between plants also permits air to circulate freely around them—an important means of preventing mildew and fungus diseases, particularly in hot and humid or damp and foggy climates.

For tips on how to thin, see page 28.

Most plants can be thinned as soon as they are big enough to grasp between your thumb and forefinger, or at least when they develop their second set of true leaves. (True leaves are those which have the leaf shape characteristic of the plant; most plants form an earlier set of seed

leaves, or cotyledons, which look different). It is best to thin as early as possible. Salad crops can be thinned twice, and the second, larger thinnings tossed into salads.

Caring for New Plants

Giving seedlings and new transplants some special care can help them get off to a good start in the garden. To make it easier for them to send new roots out into the soil that will enable them to start growing quickly, keep the soil around new transplants and seedlings evenly moist, especially for the first week or two. Even moisture helps seeds to germinate more quickly, as well, because seeds must absorb enough moisture to break their dormancy before they can begin to grow. "Evenly moist" means about as wet as a wrung-out washcloth; it does not mean soggy.

In gardens where the new plants are exposed to intense, hot sunlight—such as gardens in warm climates, or where you are planting in midsummer farther north—it is very helpful to give young seedlings and new transplants some shade as they establish themselves. The easiest way to provide shade is with shade cloth or row covers made of landscape fabric, which you should be able to find at a local garden center. Or you could stretch cheesecloth above the plants, holding it away from their leaves with stakes or wire hoops. Shade can also be used to extend the harvest of spring salad greens into summer, by keeping the soil cooler and postponing the plants' urge to bolt to seed as temperatures climb.

When the plants are six inches high and settled into the garden environment, you can mulch them to conserve moisture and help moderate soil temperatures.

Begin planting bare-root stock as soon as soil thaws. Prune conifers. Paint white or wrap trunks of young trees to prevent sunscald. Water new plants deeply if weather is dry. Layer shrubs when soil is workable.	*1-3*
Begin planting bare-root stock when soil is workable. Prune conifers. When established trees and shrubs show new growth, prune visible winter damage. Paint white or wrap trunks of young trees to prevent sunscald. Water new plants deeply in dry weather. Fertilize new plants after roots are established and they begin to grow. Layer shrubs when soil is workable.	*4*
Plant nursery stock. Prune conifers. When established trees and shrubs show new growth, prune winter damage that now becomes visible. Fertilize and mulch broad-leaved evergreens. Fertilize established trees, shrubs, and vines; fertilize new plants after roots are established and they begin to grow. Layer shrubs when soil is workable.	*5*
Finish planting bare-root stock; plant balled-and-burlapped and container-grown stock. Prune conifers. When established trees and shrubs show new growth, prune winter damage that now becomes visible. Prune spring-blooming shrubs when they finish flowering. Fertilize established trees, shrubs, and vines; fertilize new plants after roots are established and they begin to grow. Set up supports for woody vines. Watch for pests and disease symptoms.	*6*
Plant balled-and-burlapped and container-grown stock. Prune spring-blooming shrubs when they finish flowering. Fertilize established trees, shrubs, and vines if not done last month; fertilize new plants after roots are established and they begin to grow. Set up supports for woody vines. Watch for pests and disease symptoms.	*7*
Plant container-grown stock. Prune spring-blooming shrubs when they finish flowering. Pick up fallen camellia flowers; mulch camellias and other broad-leaved evergreens. Shear hedges if needed. Fasten climbers to their supports. Fertilize new plants when they begin to grow. Watch for pests and disease symptoms.	*8*
Plant container-grown stock and subtropical plants. Prune conifers in active growth. Prune spring bloomers when finished flowering. Mulch broad-leaved evergreens; pick up dropped camellia flowers. Shear hedges. Water new plants weekly, others as necessary. Fertilize new plants when they begin to grow. Watch for pests and disease symptoms. Layer or take softwood cuttings from established trees, shrubs, and vines.	*9*
See Zone 9	*10-11*

1-3

Gradually remove winter protection as soil thaws.

4

Gradually remove winter protection as soil thaws. Plant bare-root stock as soon as soil is workable; mound soil one foot high around base of new plant, remove when plant starts growing. Watch for disease symptoms when leaves begin to grow.

When soil is workable, plant ground covers, seed new lawns. De-thatch lawn if necessary, when soil is dry enough to walk on. Fertilize lawn lightly or top-dress with compost when it begins to grow.

5

Plant bare-root stock as soon as soil is workable; mound soil one foot high around base of new plant, remove when plant starts growing. Remove winter protection from established roses as soil thaws. Fertilize roses when they start to grow; feed monthly if using water-soluble fertilizer. Water weekly if weather is dry. Watch for disease symptoms when leaves begin to grow.

When soil is workable, plant ground covers, seed new lawns. Clean up lawn, aerate, de-thatch if necessary; fertilize lightly or top-dress with compost when grass begins to grow. Divide crowded ornamental grasses.

6

Plant bare-root stock when soil is workable. Remove winter protection from established roses. Fertilize roses when they start to grow; repeat monthly if using water-soluble fertilizer. Water weekly if weather is dry. Watch for disease symptoms when leaves begin to grow.

See Zone 5

7

Plant container-grown roses. Fertilize roses when they start to grow; repeat monthly if using water-soluble fertilizer. Water weekly if weather is dry. Watch for pests and disease symptoms.

Plant ground covers, seed new lawns. Finish lawn cleanup; aerate, de-thatch if necessary. Fertilize lightly or top-dress with compost. Begin mowing lawn when grass is three inches high. Water if weather is dry.

8

Plant container-grown roses. Fertilize roses when they start to grow; repeat monthly if using water-soluble fertilizer. Water weekly if weather is dry. Mulch or keep weeded. Deadhead faded flowers; cut back to nearest five-part leaf. Watch for pests and disease symptoms.

Plant ground covers. Finish lawn cleanup; aerate, de-thatch if necessary. Fertilize lightly again or top-dress with compost. Fertilize established ground covers or top-dress with compost. Mow lawn when necessary. Water if weather is dry.

9

Fertilize monthly. Water weekly if weather is dry. Mulch or keep weeded. Deadhead faded flowers; cut back to nearest five-part leaf. Watch for pests and disease symptoms.

Fertilize lawn lightly again or top-dress with compost. Fertilize established ground covers or top-dress with compost. Mow lawn when necessary. Water if weather is dry. Pull weeds from ground covers.

10-11

See Zone 9

See Zone 9

When soil becomes workable, dig and divide summer bloomers.

See Zone 3

When soil is workable plant new perennials. Dig, divide, and transplant crowded clumps of established perennials blooming in summer and fall. Fertilize new plants when they begin to grow, established plants when shoots emerge from ground. Remove winter mulch.

Plant new perennials. Dig, divide, and transplant summer and fall bloomers; divide early spring perennials when they finish blooming. Fertilize new plants when they begin to grow, established plants when shoots emerge from ground (or top-dress with compost). Watch for pests and signs of disease.

Plant container-grown perennials. Dig, divide, and transplant crowded clumps of summer and fall bloomers. When mums are six inches high, pinch back tips. Fertilize or top-dress with compost new plants as they begin to grow, established plants when shoots emerge from ground. Watch for pests and signs of disease.

Plant container-grown perennials. When mums are six inches high, pinch back tips. Fertilize or top-dress with compost new plants as they begin to grow, established plants when shoots emerge from ground. Water if weather is dry. Mulch beds and borders or keep weeded. Edge beds and borders. Watch for pests and signs of disease.

Plant container-grown summer and fall bloomers. Plant tropical and subtropical species. Pinch back mums. Provide stakes for tall plants. Fertilize or top-dress with compost new plants as they begin to grow established plants when shoots emerge from ground. Water if weather is dry. Mulch beds and borders or keep weeded. Edge beds and borders. Watch for pests and disease.

Plant container-grown summer and fall bloomers. Plant tropical and subtropical species. Provide stakes for tall plants. Fertilize or top-dress with compost new plants as they begin to grow, established plants when shoots emerge from ground. Water if weather is dry. Mulch beds and borders or keep weeded. Edge gardens. Watch for pests and diseases.

1-3

Gradually remove mulch when shoots of early bulbs begin to grow. Fertilize as growth gets underway.

Sow summer annuals indoors. Care for plants started from cuttings and seeds now growing indoors.

4

Take note of places that are sunny now but might not be later in the year—they may be good places to plant bulbs in fall. Fertilize spring bulbs as growth gets under way. Remove mulch as shoots of bulbs push through soil.

Direct-sow sweet peas as soon as soil is workable. Sow flowering cabbage or kale indoors or in cold frame to have plants to put out in late summer. Sow tender annuals indoors. Care for plants started from cuttings and seeds now growing indoors.

5

Plant and transplant true lilies, lily-of-the-valley. Fertilize bulbs as they finish blooming; deadhead, but leave foliage in place. Plant tuberous begonias, caladiums, dahlias indoors to transplant out after danger of frost is past.

Direct-sow sweet peas as soon as soil is workable. Sow flowering cabbage or kale indoors or in cold frame to have plants for fall. Plant pansies outdoors. Sow remaining summer annuals indoors. Care for plants started from cuttings and seeds now growing indoors.

6

Plant and transplant true lilies, lily-of-the-valley. Fertilize bulbs as they finish blooming; deadhead, but leave foliage in place. Start tuberous begonias, caladiums, dahlias indoors.

Direct-sow or transplant out hardy annuals. Plant out pansies. Sow remaining summer annuals indoors. Make sure sweet peas already in ground have supports. Care for plants started from cuttings and seeds now growing indoors.

7

Plant or divide and transplant true lilies, lily-of-the-valley. Plant gladiolus every two to three weeks. Begin planting dahlias. Fertilize bulbs as they finish blooming; deadhead, but leave foliage in place. Take note of places you want to plant bulbs in fall and prepare orders.

Direct-sow or transplant out hardy annuals. Sow remaining summer annuals indoors. Make sure sweet peas already in ground have supports. Thin hardy annuals planted earlier. Care for plants started from cuttings and seeds now growing indoors.

8

Plant summer bulbs; fertilize when shoots appear. Fertilize spring bulbs when they finish blooming; deadhead, but leave foliage in place. Divide and transplant crowded clumps of bulbs when leaves yellow. Take note of places you want to plant bulbs in fall and prepare orders.

Direct-sow or transplant out tender annuals when danger of frost is past. Fertilize outdoor plants with liquid fertilizer. Water and weed as needed. Deadhead faded flowers.

9

Plant summer bulbs; fertilize when shoots appear. Divide and transplant crowded clumps of spring bulbs when leaves yellow. Fertilize spring bulbs when they finish blooming; deadhead, but leave foliage in place. Take note of places you want to plant bulbs in fall and prepare orders.

Direct-sow or transplant out tender annuals when danger of frost is past. Feed outdoor plants with liquid fertilizer. Water and weed as needed. Edge beds and borders. Pull up winter annuals when plants fatigue; put on compost pile.

10-11

Plant summer bulbs; fertilize when shoots appear. Fertilize spring bulbs when leaves yellow; deadhead, but leave foliage in place. Divide and transplant crowded clumps of spring bulbs when they finish blooming. Take note of places you want to plant bulbs and prepare orders.

Direct-sow or transplant out tender annuals. Feed outdoor plants with liquid fertilizer. Water and weed as needed. Edge beds and borders. Pull up winter annuals when plants fatigue; put on compost pile. Watch for pests and signs of disease.

Container Gardens

Vegetables & Herbs

Container Gardens	Vegetables & Herbs	Zone
Check tender container plants moved indoors for winter.	Prepare soil for early planting; cover with black plastic for several sunny days, then dig. Turn compost pile when it thaws. Spread wood ashes over garden to melt snow. Care for plants growing indoors: adjust lights, turn windowsill seedlings daily.	1-3
See Zone 3	Plant out spring vegetables when heavy frost is over. Protect young seedlings with hot caps or plastic tunnels on cold nights. Finish sowing summer vegetables and tender herbs indoors early this month. If cutworms are a problem, place collars around seedlings. Turn compost pile when it thaws. Care for seedlings growing indoors.	4
Plan container plantings for decks, patios, and other places. Check tender container plants moved indoors for winter.	Direct-sow or plant out cold-tolerant vegetables and herbs when heavy frost is over; direct-sow peas as soon as soil is workable. Sow tender herbs indoors early this month. Place cutworm collars around seedlings if needed. Turn compost pile. Care for seedlings growing indoors.	5
See Zone 5	Harvest early asparagus when ready; harvest salad crops from cold frame. Direct-sow or plant out cold-tolerant vegetables and herbs. Place cutworm collars around seedlings if needed. Open cold frame on mild days. Turn compost pile. Care for seedlings growing indoors.	6
Plan container plantings for decks, patio, and other places. Begin planting containers of cold-tolerant vegetables and annuals, small shrubs and small trees. Check tender container plants moved indoors for winter; move out after danger of frost is past.	Harvest asparagus, spinach, and early salad crops. Direct-sow or plant out successions of cold-tolerant vegetables and herbs. Thin seedlings of earlier plantings. Water garden if weather is dry. Place cutworm collars around seedlings if needed. Open cold frame on mild days. Turn compost pile. Care for seedlings growing indoors.	7
Plant containers of vegetables and annuals, small shrubs and small trees. When danger of frost is past, plant tender container plants, and move tender plants brought indoors for winter back outdoors. Water new plantings as needed; feed with liquid fertilizer.	Harvest early crops. Direct-sow or plant out successions of cold-tolerant vegetables and herbs. Plant out tender crops when danger of frost is past. Feed seedlings with liquid fertilizer after planting. Thin seedlings of earlier plantings. Water if weather is dry. Weed as needed. Turn compost pile. Watch for pests and signs of disease.	8
Plant containers of summer vegetables, tender herbs, and flowers when danger of frost is past. Move tender plants brought indoors for winter back outdoors. Water container plantings as needed. Feed with liquid fertilizer. Put supports in place for climbers.	Harvest early crops. Direct-sow or plant out successions of cold-tolerant vegetables. Plant tender vegetables and herbs when danger of frost is past. Feed seedlings with liquid fertilizer after planting. Thin seedlings of earlier plantings. Water if weather is dry. Weed as needed. Put up stakes and supports for plants that will need them. Turn compost pile. Watch for pests and signs of disease.	9
Plant containers of summer vegetables, tender herbs, and flowers. Water container plantings as needed. Feed with liquid fertilizer. Put supports in place for climbers. Watch for pests and signs of disease.	Direct-sow or plant out tender vegetables and herbs. Feed seedlings with liquid fertilizer after planting. Thin seedlings from earlier plantings. Water if weather is dry. Mulch when plants are tall enough. Put up stakes and supports for plants that will need them. Turn compost pile. Watch for pests and signs of disease.	10-11

1-3 Plant fruit trees, bushes, and brambles when soil is workable. Paint white or wrap trunks of young trees to prevent sunscald. Fertilize established berries and grapes or top-dress with compost. Water new plantings deeply if weather is dry.

4 Plant fruit trees, bushes, and brambles when soil is workable. Paint white or wrap trunks of young trees to prevent sunscald. Fertilize established berries and grapes or top-dress with compost. Water new plantings deeply in dry weather. Stake brambles. When heavy frost is past, remove mulches from established plants. Check for borers and caterpillars on trees; take appropriate measures.

5 When heavy frost is past, remove mulches from established plants; fertilize or top-dress with compost. Water new plantings if weather is dry. Stake brambles. Check for borers and caterpillars on trees.

6 Remove mulches from established plants; fertilize or top-dress with compost. Water new plantings if weather is dry. Thin brambles if needed; stake plants. Stake newly planted stock that needs it. Fasten grape stems to training wires. Remove flowers from newly planted strawberries. Watch for borers and caterpillars on trees.

7 Remove mulches from established plants; fertilize or top-dress with compost. Water new plantings if weather is dry. Thin brambles if needed; stake plants. Stake newly planted stock that needs it. Fasten grape stems to training wires. Remove flowers from newly planted strawberries. Watch for pests. Watch for signs of fire blight; prune affected branches and dispose of them.

8 Water strawberries and newly planted stock. Pinch off runners on new strawberry plants. Mulch bushes, trees, and strawberries. Thin citrus fruit. Cover berries with netting to keep away birds. Watch for pests and signs of disease; prune and dispose of branches with fire blight.

9 Plant tropical fruits. Fertilize fruit trees again. Stake brambles. Thin citrus fruit, apples, and peaches. Cover berries with netting to keep away birds. Watch for signs of pests and disease; prune and dispose of branches with fire blight.

10-11 Plant tropical fruits. Fertilize fruit trees again. Water newly planted stock deeply in dry weather. Stake brambles. Thin citrus fruit, apples, and peaches. Cover berries with netting to keep away birds. Watch for signs of pests and disease.

How to Sow Seeds

Very small seeds, like those of wax begonias, coleus, or lisianthus, are difficult to handle. To make it easier to sow them evenly, mix the seeds with an equal volume of fine sand, and scatter the mixture over the top of the potting medium (indoors) or in a prepared drill or across the surface of the bed (outdoors). Another method is to place the seeds in a folded piece of paper and tap them out one at a time onto the soil.

To sow somewhat larger seeds, such as those of eggplant, broadcast them over the top of the soil or potting medium, or release them from your hand between your thumb and forefinger to drop them into drills. Cover the seeds to the proper depth.

Scatter large seeds over the surface of the soil or plant them in rows or whatever pattern you like, at the depth recommended on the seed packet.

Tips on Thinning

Thinning is easiest when soil is moist. To thin, grasp the leaves gently between your thumb and forefinger and lift the seedling out of the ground. If the plants are tiny, use a tweezers to pull them up. If the seedlings are very crowded, use a cuticle scissors to cut the stems of the ones you don't want, to avoid damaging the roots of nearby plants that you wish to leave in place.

If removing any plants loosens the soil, pat back in place.

May

About Fertilizers

As the weather warms and plants are growing actively, gardeners turn their attention to maintaining the plants in peak condition. Along with watering (which is discussed on page 36), fertilizing and mulching are basic maintenance chores for most gardeners.

Fertilizers are sources of minerals that nourish plants. The major nutrients important to plants are nitrogen (N), phosphorus (P), and potassium (K). In addition, an array of secondary minerals known as trace elements, such as calcium, iron, boron, and magnesium, is needed for good plant growth.

Each nutrient has a particular role to play. Nitrogen promotes photosynthesis and healthy leaves, and is especially valuable for lawn grasses, foliage ornamentals, salad greens, and other leafy plants. Phosphorus assists plants in forming flowers, ripening seeds and fruit, and growing roots. Potassium enhances overall plant vigor and fruit formation, and is considered important for tubers and root crops.

Fertilizers take several forms. The term "organic" is widely used to describe materials used as nutrient sources in a more-or-less natural form. They decompose slowly in the soil to release nutrients for plants. It may take months for nutrients from organic materials to become available to plants.

Organic materials were traditionally supplied individually; gardeners would dig animal manures, rock powders, seaweed, wood ashes, and other materials into the soil. Now organic fertilizers are also available in granular or powdered form, in packaged, preblended formulations. If you opt for a convenient, packaged organic plant food, read the label carefully to be sure the nutrients are really supplied by organic materials.

Compost (described on page x) is an excellent soil conditioner and source of organic matter, but is not in itself considered a fertilizer. However, if compost is supplied in substantial amounts over a period of years to build soil to excellent condition, no additional fertilizer will be necessary for many plants.

The term "chemical fertilizer" usually refers to fertilizers that are synthesized, or whose form is somehow altered from the way it occurs in nature. Many are made from petroleum derivatives. Chemical fertilizers are generally far more concentrated than organics, and their nutrients very quickly become available to plants (unless the product is a timed-release formula). Like the newer organic blends, chemical fertilizers are widely available in granular or powdered form to be worked into the soil around plants.

Follow package directions explicitly when using any fertilizers, especially chemical formulas. Overfertilizing causes rapid but weak growth that is highly susceptible to diseases and damage from pests. In the case of concentrated chemical fertilizers, overuse or incorrect application can actually cause the fertilizer to burn plant tissues. Also, runoff from excessive applications of fertilizers (and pesticides) is a major source of groundwater pollution, particularly in agricultural areas, and home gardeners should not contribute to the problem.

Water-soluble fertilizers are often used to get new transplants off to a rousing start, and also offer a convenient way to fertilize plants growing in containers. Water-soluble fertilizers are dissolved in or diluted with water, and then applied to the soil for roots to absorb, or sprayed onto leaves (a process known as foliar feeding). Liquid fertilizers can be used in mild form, diluted to one-half or one-quarter the recommended strength, to feed young seedlings. Water-soluble fertilizers are available in various formulas. Organic gardeners can mix their own liquid plant foods with fish emulsion, seaweed solutions, or water in which manure or compost has been soaked.

An all-purpose fertilizer formula, which contains relatively balanced amounts of nitrogen, phosphorus, and potassium, will be useful for a variety of plants. For flowering plants, fruits, and vegetables that bear their crops in the form of fruit (tomatoes, cucumbers, peas, and beans, for example) or tuberous roots (carrots, potatoes), use a fertilizer higher in phosphorus and potassium than in nitrogen. Flowering bulbs also need these nutrients. Organic sources of phosphorus are bone meal, colloidal phosphate, and phosphate rock; wood ashes, greensand, and granite dust supply potassium.

Foliage plants, such as hostas and salad greens, need a formula rich in nitrogen. Organic gardeners can add animal manures, cottonseed meal, fish products, or dried blood to their soil to supply nitrogen.

Trace elements are important, too. Good organic sources are seaweed and algae products.

Lawn fertilizers are probably more widely available than any other kind. It is a fairly simple matter to select a chemical lawn fertilizer from the shelf at the garden center. If you prefer to care for your lawn organically, you can top-dress it twice a year with compost and composted manure that has been finely crumbled or pushed through a coarse sieve.

Some plants have special needs for fertilizing. Acid-

loving plants such as azaleas need to have nutrients supplied in a special form, in order for their roots to be able to use them readily. For azaleas, rhododendrons, camellias, blueberries, hollies, and other acid-loving plants, look for fertilizers specially formulated for their needs.

About Mulches

Mulch is a material used to cover and insulate the soil around and between plants. Mulches can be of organic or inorganic materials.

Organic mulches include dry leaves (preferably shredded), straw, salt hay, cocoa bean hulls, wood chips, shredded bark, and sawdust. Organic mulches are widely used and some of them are quite attractive in the garden. They serve different functions depending on the time of year.

In summer, mulches slow the evaporation of water from the soil, keep soil temperatures cooler, and discourage weed growth by cutting off the light that encourages weed seeds in the soil to germinate. Under the mulch the soil surface stays loose and crumbly, making it easy to remove whatever weeds do sprout. Lay summer mulch after the soil has warmed in spring, and when plants are at least six inches tall. Apply finer-textured materials such as cocoa hulls about two inches deep, coarser materials such as straw four to six inches deep.

These materials will decompose over a period of time and add organic matter to the soil. Sawdust and other wood products will use nitrogen as they decompose, so add extra nitrogen to the soil to compensate for the loss. If your garden suffers a lot of problems from slugs, you may wish to forgo the mulch—mulches offer an ideal hiding place for slugs during the day, and may increase their populations in your garden.

In winter, organic mulches insulate the soil and help to keep it frozen during spells of mild weather, so that plant roots are less likely to be damaged during alternate periods of freezing and thawing. Cycles of freezing and thawing can cause soil to heave and buckle, and the roots of dormant perennials and roses can be forced right out of the ground. Exposed roots are likely to be killed by freezing or drying out. Apply winter mulches six to twelve inches deep.

Stones or pebbles can also be used as mulch. Like other organic mulches, they conserve moisture and keep down weeds, but they have the added ability to absorb warmth from the sun during the day and release it slowly at night. You must decide if this would be a burden or blessing in your garden.

An inorganic mulch can be created with black plastic. Black plastic mulch is excellent for suppressing weeds. If the idea of a plastic mulch appeals to you, be aware that it also holds heat in the ground, and indeed, can cause soil to become quite warm. When installing the mulch, take care to leave large enough holes around plants to permit moisture to penetrate to the roots; otherwise the plants will dehydrate. You will also find black plastic more aesthetically pleasing if you cover it with wood chips or other material.

Plant trees and shrubs; water well; mulch after soil is warm. Prune winter-damaged growth and wood damaged by late frost. Check for borers and other pests.

Finish planting bare-root stock early in month. Plant balled-and-burlapped and container-grown stock. Water new plants well and mulch when soil is warm. Prune winter-damaged growth and wood damaged by late frost. Check for borers and other pests.

Plant evergreens, container-grown trees, and shrubs. Water well and mulch new plants. Prune spring-flowering shrubs after bloom; prune conifers in active growth. Fertilize after pruning. Begin watering if weather is dry. Watch for pests and signs of disease.

Plant container-grown stock. Mulch new plants. Prune spring-flowering shrubs after bloom; prune conifers in active growth. Fertilize after pruning. Begin watering if weather is dry. Watch for pests and signs of disease.

Plant container-grown stock. Mulch new plants; use acid material for acid lovers. Prune spring bloomers when they finish flowering; cut pussy willow back to a few inches above ground. Prune conifers in active growth. Train new shoots of clematis and other climbers; thin if necessary. Fertilize after pruning. Begin watering in dry weather. Watch for pests and signs of disease.

Plant balled-and-burlapped and container-grown stock if weather is not yet too hot. Mulch new and established plants. Prune spring bloomers when they finish flowering; prune conifers in active growth. Trim hedges if needed. Begin watering if weather is dry. Watch for pests and signs of disease. Take softwood cuttings.

Plant container-grown stock, including palms. Deadhead and prune late-spring-flowering shrubs when they finish blooming. Prune tropical and subtropical plants. Trim topiaries and espaliers. Take softwood cuttings from deciduous trees and shrubs and broad-leaved evergreens. Watch for pests and signs of disease.

Plant container-grown stock, including tropical and subtropical plants. Deadhead and prune late spring-blooming shrubs when they finish flowering. Prune subtropical and tropical plants. Trim topiaries and espaliers. Take softwood cuttings from deciduous trees and shrubs and broad-leaved evergreens.

If late frost strikes, prune damaged new growth from shrub roses. Plant bare-root stock when soil is workable; mound soil one foot high around base of plant, remove when plant starts growing.	Plant ground covers. Seed new lawns; overseed bare spots. When soil is dry enough to walk on, aerate lawn and de-thatch if necessary. Fertilize lawn lightly or top-dress with compost. Begin mowing lawn when grass is three inches high.	*1–3*
If late frost strikes, prune damaged new growth. Plant bare-root roses when soil is workable; mound soil one foot high around base of plant, remove when plant starts growing. Watch for disease symptoms when leaves begin to grow.	Plant ground covers. Seed new lawns; overseed bare spots. If not done last month, aerate lawn and de-thatch if necessary. Begin mowing lawn when grass is three inches high.	*4*
Plant container-grown stock. Deadhead faded flowers. Fertilize. Water once a week if weather is dry. Mulch plants when soil warms. Watch for pests and signs of disease.	Plant ground covers and ornamental grasses. Pull weeds from ground covers. Begin mowing lawn when grass is three inches high.	*5*
Plant container-grown stock. Deadhead faded flowers; cut back to a five-part leaf. Fertilize. Water once a week if weather is dry. Mulch plants when soil warms. Watch for pests and signs of disease.	See Zone 5	*6*
See Zone 6	Plant ground covers and ornamental grasses. Pull weeds from ground covers. Water lawn and new plants weekly in dry weather. Mow lawn as needed.	*7*
Finish planting container-grown roses. Deadhead faded flowers; cut back to a five-part leaf. Prune climbers when finished blooming. Fertilize. Water once a week or as needed if weather is dry. Watch for pests and signs of disease.	Finish planting ground covers and ornamental grasses. In southern areas, seed or sod summer lawn grasses. Water established lawns weekly in dry weather, new plants and seeded areas as needed. Mow lawn as needed.	*8*
Deadhead faded flowers; cut back to a five-part leaf. Prune climbers and ramblers when finished blooming. Fertilize. Water once a week or as needed if weather is dry. Watch for pests and signs of disease.	Seed or sod summer lawn grasses. Water established lawns weekly in dry weather, new plants and seeded areas as needed. Mow lawn as needed.	*9*
See Zone 9	See Zone 9	*10–11*

Perennials

Bulbs

1-3

When soil is workable plant new perennials. Dig and divide crowded summer bloomers.

Fertilize late spring bulbs as they begin to grow. Weed bulb beds.

4

Sow perennials and biennials in cold frame for plants to set in garden next year. Plant new perennials when soil is workable. Fertilize spring bloomers as they begin to grow.

Prepare soil for planting summer bulbs. Fertilize late bulbs as they begin to grow. Deadhead spring bloomers when flowers fade; leave foliage in place. Weed bulb beds.

5

Sow perennials and biennials in cold frame for plants to set in garden next year. Plant new perennials. Fertilize spring bloomers when they start to grow. Weed beds and borders. Water if needed. Edge gardens. Pinch mums when six inches high. Divide mums and other late bloomers; divide early spring bloomers when they finish flowering.

Prepare soil for planting summer bulbs; plant out when all danger of frost is past and soil is warm. Fertilize late spring bulbs as they begin to grow. Weed bulb beds. Deadhead spring bloomers when flowers fade; leave foliage in place.

6

Plant new perennials. Fertilize established plants when they begin to grow. Weed beds and borders. Water if needed. Edge gardens. Pinch mums when six inches high. Divide mums and other late bloomers; divide early bloomers when they finish flowering. Watch for pests and signs of disease.

Plant summer bulbs when all danger of frost is past and soil is warm. Fertilize late spring bulbs as they begin to grow. Weed bulb beds. Deadhead spring bloomers when flowers fade; leave foliage in place.

7

Plant container-grown perennials. Fertilize established plants when they begin to grow. Weed beds and borders. Water when needed, especially plants with buds or flowers. Edge gardens. Deadhead faded flowers. Pinch mums. Divide early bloomers when they finish flowering. Watch for pests and signs of disease.

Plant out summer bulbs when all danger of frost is past and soil is warm. Divide lily-of-the-valley after bloom; transplant other spring bloomers after bloom but before foliage dies. Tie up floppy daffodil leaves with rubber bands to control them. Put stakes in place for tall dahlias and gladiolus. Weed bulbs. Deadhead spring bloomers when flowers fade; leave foliage in place.

8

Plant container-grown perennials; protect new plants with shade cloth. Weed beds and borders if not mulched. Water when needed, especially plants with buds or flowers. Deadhead faded flowers. Pinch back mums. Watch for pests and signs of disease.

Plant summer bulbs. Divide and transplant crowded spring bloomers after bloom but before foliage dies. Dig and discard tulips and hyacinths or store the bulbs to replant in fall. Fertilize summer bulbs as they begin to grow. Tie up floppy daffodil leaves with rubber bands to control them. Put stakes in place for tall dahlias and gladiolus. Deadhead spring bloomers when flowers fade; leave foliage in place.

9

Plant container-grown perennials and cacti; protect new plants with shade cloth. Weed gardens if not mulched. Water regularly, especially plants with buds or flowers. Deadhead faded flowers. Pinch back mums. Watch for pests and signs of disease.

Divide and transplant crowded narcissus after bloom but before foliage dies. Dig and discard or store hyacinths and tulips after bloom. Fertilize summer bulbs. Put stakes in place for tall dahlias and gladiolus.

10-11 See Zone 9

Divide and transplant crowded narcissus after bloom but before foliage dies. Dig and discard or store hyacinths and tulips after bloom. Put stakes in place for tall dahlias and gladiolus.

Annuals

Notes

Direct-sow or plant out hardy annuals when danger of heavy frost is past. Prepare soil for future planting.

Direct-sow or plant out hardy annuals when danger of heavy frost is past. Plant out seedlings of summer annuals when all danger of frost is past.

Direct-sow or plant out hardy annuals when danger of heavy frost is past. Plant out seedlings of summer annuals when all danger of frost is past. Feed new transplants with liquid fertilizer.

Plant hardy annuals. Direct-sow or transplant out tender annuals when all danger of frost is past. Fertilize new transplants with liquid fertilizer. Edge beds and borders. Weed and water if necessary.

Plant tender annuals when frost danger is past. Plant annuals around spring bulbs to hide foliage. Feed new transplants and sweet peas with liquid fertilizer. Weed and water if necessary. Keep sweet peas fastened to supports; mulch well. Edge beds and borders.

Plant tender annuals. Fertilize new transplants with liquid fertilizer. Water in dry weather. Weed as necessary. Dead-head faded flowers. Pull early annuals as plants fatigue; replace with summer bloomers. Edge beds and borders. Watch for pests and signs of disease.

Plant tender annuals. Feed new transplants with liquid fertilizer. Mulch or keep weeded. Water in dry weather. Put stakes in place for tall plants. Train annual vines on trellises or other supports. Deadhead faded flowers. Pull spent plants and replace with summer bloomers. Cut back sweet alyssum and petunias to stimulate more bloom. Watch for pests and signs of disease.

See Zone 9

1-3

Set out transplants of pansies and cool-weather vegetables in containers when danger of heavy frost is past. Check tender container plants moved indoors for winter.

Sow or plant out cool-weather crops when soil begins to warm. Mulch when plants are several inches high. Turn compost pile when it thaws.

4

Set out transplants of pansies and cool-weather vegetables in containers when danger of heavy frost is past. Feed new plants with liquid fertilizer. Check tender container plants moved indoors for winter.

Sow or plant out cool-weather crops when soil begins to warm. Thin seedlings sown earlier. Mulch when plants are several inches high. Set out transplants or warm-weather crops when all danger of frost is past. Put supports in place for peas. Turn compost pile. Watch for insects and signs of disease.

5

Set out transplants of pansies and cool-weather vegetables, small shrubs and small trees in containers when danger of heavy frost is past. Feed new plants with liquid fertilizer. Check tender container plants moved indoors for winter.

When danger of heavy frost is past, sow or plant out cool-weather crops and set out transplants of warm-weather crops. Thin and fertilize seedlings sown earlier. Mulch when plants are several inches high. Weed if needed. Turn compost pile. Watch for insects and signs of disease.

6

Plant summer container plants when danger of frost is past. Feed new transplants with liquid fertilizer. Water when needed. When frost danger is past, move back outdoors tender container plants kept indoors over winter.

Harvest asparagus and early crops from cold frame. Sow or plant out successions of early crops. Plant warm-weather crops and tender herbs when all danger of frost is past. Thin and fertilize seedlings sown earlier. Weed and water as needed. Edge garden. Turn compost pile. Watch for pests and signs of disease.

7

Plant summer container plants when danger of frost is past. Feed new transplants with liquid fertilizer. Water as needed. Deadhead faded flowers of earlier plantings.

Harvest early crops. As asparagus harvest ends, cut back female plants with berries. Plant successions of early crops. Plant warm-weather crops and tender herbs. Thin and fertilize seedlings sown earlier. When peas stop producing, cut vines to ground (do not pull); replace with summer crops. Weed and water as needed. Edge garden. Turn compost pile. Watch for pests and signs of disease.

8

Plant summer container plants when danger of frost is past. Feed new transplants with liquid fertilizer. Water as needed. Deadhead faded flowers of earlier plantings. Watch for pests and signs of disease.

Harvest early crops. Sow or plant out warm-weather crops and tender herbs. Thin and fertilize seedlings sown earlier. Put stakes, poles, and trellises in place for tall and climbing crops. Weed and water as needed. Edge garden. Turn compost pile. Watch for pests and signs of disease.

9

Water container plants daily or as needed. Feed with liquid fertilizer. Deadhead faded flowers. Watch for pests and signs of disease.

Harvest early crops. Plant successions of warm-weather crops. Thin and fertilize seedlings sown earlier. Put stakes, poles, and trellises in place for tall and climbing crops. Weed and water as needed. Edge garden. Turn compost pile. Watch for pests and signs of disease.

10-11 See Zone 9

See Zone 9

Fruit

Plant fruit trees, bushes, and brambles when soil is workable. Paint white or wrap trunks of young trees to prevent sunscald. Fertilize or top-dress with compost established berries and grapes if not done last month. Water new plantings deeply if weather is dry.

Cover strawberries if late frost is possible. Thin brambles. Thin fruit on apples, pears, and plums when marble-size. Replace mulches removed last month. Prune suckers and water sprouts from trees. Fertilize or top-dress with compost established berries and grapes if not done last month. Water new plantings deeply if weather is dry. Watch for pests and signs of disease.

Cover strawberries if late frost is possible. Thin brambles. Thin fruit on apples, peaches, pears, and plums when marble-size. Replace mulches removed last month. Prune suckers and water sprouts from trees. Water new plantings deeply if weather is dry. Watch for pests and signs of disease.

Thin fruit on apples, peaches, pears, and plums when marble-size. Replace mulches removed last month. Prune suckers and water sprouts from trees, weak shoots from brambles. Water new plantings deeply if weather is dry. Watch for pests and signs of disease. Trap larvae on trunks of trees and destroy.

Harvest strawberries as they ripen. Thin fruit on apples, peaches, pears, and plums when marble-size. Replace mulches removed last month. Remove weak shoots from brambles. Water new plantings deeply if weather is dry. Watch for pests and signs of disease. Trap larvae on tree trunks and destroy. Prune wood damaged by fire blight.

Harvest strawberries as they ripen. Thin fruit on apples, peaches, pears, and plums when marble-size. Replace mulches removed last month. Fertilize grapes. Water deeply if weather is dry. Watch for pests and signs of disease. Trap and destroy larvae on tree trunks. Prune wood damaged by fire blight.

Harvest strawberries. Plant citrus. Fertilize new plantings and grapes. Water deeply in dry weather. Watch for pests and signs of disease. Cover berries with netting to protect them from birds.

Plant citrus and tropical fruit. Fertilize new plantings and grapes. Water deeply in dry weather. Cover berries with netting to protect them from birds. Watch for pests and signs of disease.

Organic Nutrient Sources

Apply these materials to your garden in combinations of your choice, or look for them on the labels of packaged, preblended organic fertilizers.

Nitrogen Sources
Blood meal or dried blood
Bone meal (small amount of nitrogen)
Coffee grounds
Cottonseed meal (good for acid-loving plants)
Fish emulsion, fish meal
Manures (chicken, cow, horse, sheep, zoo animals)
Soybean meal

Phosphorus Sources
Blood meal or dried blood (small amount of phosphorus)
Bone meal
Colloidal phosphate
Fish emulsion, fish meal (small amount of phosphorus)
Mushroom compost (available from commercial mushroom farms)
Phosphate rock

Potassium Sources
Fish emulsion, fish meal (small amount of phosphorus)
Granite dust
Greensand
Seaweed
Wood ashes

Organic gardeners can obtain trace elements from such sources as kelp and other seaweed, and chelated minerals. Epsom salts supply magnesium, and household borax can be used to correct boron deficiencies.

June

Watering

June ushers in warm weather in many parts of North America. In southern zones, temperatures are getting quite hot. Even in the far North the weather is moderating. With the mercury climbing and so many plants in active growth, gardeners must be ready to supply the garden with water when nature does not.

All plants must have water in order to grow. Water fuels photosynthesis, and is the medium through which dissolved mineral nutrients are carried into plants through their roots. But how much water is necessary, and how often it is needed, varies tremendously among plants. Aquatic plants like water lilies must have their roots continually moist. At the other extreme, cacti can survive for months with no water at all. Most plants' water needs fall somewhere in between.

It is important to learn when your plants need to be watered. The traditional rule of thumb is to make sure the garden gets one inch of water each week during the growing season; if rainfall is insufficient the gardener must supply the difference. But this maxim is just an average; it is not an accurate guide for all plants in all soils and climates. A garden in a coastal location where the soil is sandy and the summer sun is hot will need more than one inch of water per week. Plants growing in a cool, foggy climate

or in dense clay soil will need less than an inch. Instead of leaving the timer on the automatic watering system on the same setting all summer, or watering every Wednesday and Saturday without fail, try to water your plants when *they* need it.

For plants in beds and borders, the best way to tell when it is time to water is to poke a finger into the soil. Don't just lay your hand on the soil surface; the soil surface may be dry from the hot sun when there is still adequate moisture in the root zone. But when the ground feels dry more than an inch or two underground, watering is in order. Do not put off watering until your plants wilt or appear limp; wilting indicates severe water stress that can damage plants or at least slow their growth. Water-stressed plants will also bloom and bear fruit later and less lavishly than healthier specimens. Some plants look a bit flaccid during the hottest part of the day, especially when the sun is intense, but will revive later on, toward dusk. But if plants are limp in the morning or evening, they are suffering water stress or are beset by disease or an insect infestation. If drought is the problem, water the plants immediately.

Check the soil regularly during hot, dry weather and water when necessary to keep your plants vigorous and healthy. The need for water is most critical for many plants at different stages in their life cycle. If you live in a drought-prone area and need—or want—to conserve water, the following are the most important times to water.

All plants need water during transplanting, and until they are well established in the soil. Trees and shrubs should be watered during dry periods for the first one to two *years* after planting. Woody plants also need water when setting buds; for spring bloomers bud set occurs in late summer. Water plants to water in fertilizers, also.

Annuals and perennials need the most water during seed germination, and when setting buds. Vegetables, too, need watering from sowing until germination. After that point, leafy crops need water regularly throughout their growth; root crops need water as the roots are enlarging; and fruiting crops are most in need of water during flowering and fruit formation.

When you do water, water deeply so the moisture soaks into the soil to a depth of at least two feet. Surface water evaporates quickly, and frequent light waterings encourage plants to concentrate many roots in the upper levels of the soil, where they will be more vulnerable to hot sun and dry weather. But deep watering coaxes deep-rooted trees, shrubs, and other plants into sending roots down into the soil, where they will be able to find more moisture during dry weather. This approach saves water, because you water less often, and less of the water is lost to evaporation. Your plants will not be dependent on you to supply all the moisture they require.

One important exception to the watering rule is container plants. Because containers—even large ones—hold a relatively small volume of soil in comparison to a garden bed or border, the soil dries out quickly, especially in hot, dry weather. It is important to water container plants thoroughly—until excess water seeps from the drainage holes in the bottom of the pot. But container plants need to be watered more often than garden plants. Small pots and windowboxes need watering every day, and sometimes twice a day, in hot weather. Use the same test you use in the garden to tell when your container plants need water—stick a finger into the soil and water when it feels dry below the surface. You can also gauge dryness by the weight of a small pot or hanging basket: when it feels light, the plant needs water.

Gardeners in the Southwest and along the West Coast are well acquainted with water shortages. But the threat

of more serious and widespread water shortages hangs over all of us, and it is essential that gardeners everywhere use water as efficiently as possible to avoid wasting this precious resource.

The most efficient way to get water to plants is to supply it right at ground level, through soaker hoses or drip irrigation systems. Soaker hoses are made of porous rubber (the ones I use are made from recycled tires), canvas, or fiber. The tiny pores in the hose walls allow water to seep out slowly. The hoses can be snaked through the garden, laid right on top of the soil. Connect them to one another to get the necessary length, then connect them to a faucet with a conventional hose. To water, turn on the faucet partway for an hour or more, until the water soaks deep into the soil. It is easiest to lay soaker hoses in spring when plants are still small. If you don't like the way they look, cover them with mulch.

Drip irrigation systems are more expensive and require more work to install, but once in place they are convenient and effective. They use lengths of narrow plastic tubing with perforations along the sides. The tubing is connected by couplings, and can be hooked up to a timer to operate automatically. Drip tubing is best installed below the soil surface, which requires some digging. You can buy the components individually or in kit form. One drawback to drip systems is that they may become clogged, especially in areas where the water is hard.

The least efficient ways to water are overhead sprinklers and hoses. Watering from above is wasteful, because the water has to filter down through foliage to get to the soil, and because water is lost to evaporation on hot days. If plants are watered too late in the day, moisture that remains on leaf surfaces at night can invite the growth of mildew and fungus. However, overhead watering does offer the benefits of helping to cool plants in hot weather, and rinsing dirt from foliage. A strong spray of water from a hose can wash away aphids and other small pests, too. If you must water with a hose, the best time to do it is in the morning or late afternoon; avoid midday, when evaporation will be greatest. If you water late in the afternoon, be sure a few hours of daylight remain so that leaves will dry before dark. Another option is to get a bubbler attachment for the hose and lay it on the ground, moving it around to water different parts of the garden.

Fertilize broad-leaved evergreens when they finish blooming. Carefully work old mulch into soil; replace with fresh mulch. Deadhead and prune spring-blooming shrubs when they finish flowering. If late frost strikes, prune damaged growth. Watch for pests and signs of disease.

1-3

Fertilize broad-leaved evergreens when they finish blooming. Remove old mulches or carefully work into soil; replace with fresh mulch. Deadhead and prune spring-blooming shrubs when they finish flowering. Trim hedges and prune evergreens if needed. Watch for pests and signs of disease.

4

Plant container-grown trees and shrubs. Water new plants regularly. Fertilize broad-leaved evergreens when they finish blooming. Weed and water as needed. Deadhead and prune spring-blooming shrubs when they finish flowering. Trim hedges. Watch for pests and signs of disease.

5

Plant container-grown trees and shrubs. Water new plants regularly. Fertilize broad-leaved evergreens when they finish blooming. Weed and water established plants as needed. Deadhead and prune spring-blooming shrubs when they finish flowering. Trim hedges. Watch for pests and signs of disease.

6

Plant container-grown stock if weather is not too hot. Water new plants regularly. Fertilize broad-leaved evergreens when they finish blooming. Weed and water established plants as needed. Deadhead and prune spring-blooming shrubs when they finish flowering. Trim hedges. Watch for pests and signs of disease.

7

Fertilize broad-leaved evergreens when they finish blooming. Water new plants regularly. Weed and water established plants as needed. Deadhead and prune spring-blooming shrubs when they finish flowering. Trim vines. Prune suckers and weak or damaged wood from trees and shrubs. Keep trees mulched to about one foot from trunk. Watch for pests and signs of disease.

8

Plant container-grown subtropicals. Water new plants regularly. Weed and water established plants as needed. Fertilize tropicals and subtropicals, and broad-leaved evergreens when they finish blooming. Prune shrubs and vines when they finish flowering. Prune suckers and weak or damaged wood from trees and shrubs to prevent wind damage. Keep trees mulched to about one foot from trunk. Watch for pests and signs of disease.

9

Plant container-grown tropical and subtropical plants. Water new plants regularly and established plants as needed. Fertilize tropicals and subtropicals, and broad-leaved evergreens when they finish blooming. Prune shrubs and vines when they finish flowering. Prune suckers and weak or damaged wood from trees and shrubs. Mulch trees to about one foot from trunk. Watch for pests and disease.

10-11

1–3

Deadhead faded flowers. Fertilize roses. Water deeply during dry weather. If late frost strikes, prune damaged growth. Watch for pests and signs of disease.

Plant ground covers. Mow lawn as needed. Water weekly if weather is dry.

4

See Zone 3

See Zone 3

5

Plant container-grown roses. Deadhead faded flowers. Fertilize roses. Water deeply during dry weather. Watch for pests and signs of disease.

See Zone 3

6

See Zone 5

Plant ground covers. Mow lawn as needed. Water weekly if weather is dry. If lawn looks sparse, thin overhead tree branches, reseed with shade-tolerant grasses or replace with shade-tolerant ground cover.

7

Plant container-grown roses. Deadhead faded flowers. Prune climbers and ramblers when finished blooming. Fertilize. Water deeply during dry weather. Watch for pests and signs of disease.

See Zone 6

8

See Zone 7

Fertilize ground covers. Lightly fertilize warm-season lawn grasses. Mow lawn as needed. Water weekly if weather is dry. If lawn looks sparse, thin overhead tree branches, reseed with shade-tolerant grasses or replace with shade-tolerant ground cover.

9

Deadhead faded flowers. Prune climbers and ramblers when finished blooming. Fertilize roses. Water deeply during dry weather. Watch for pests and signs of disease.

Lightly fertilize warm-season lawn grasses. Mow lawn as needed. Water weekly if weather is dry. If lawn looks sparse, thin overhead tree branches, reseed with shade-tolerant grasses or replace with shade-tolerant ground cover.

10–11

See Zone 9

See Zone 9

Plant container-grown perennials. Fertilize perennials as they start to grow. Deadhead faded flowers on early bloomers. Weed and water as needed. Watch for pests and signs of disease.

See Zone 3

Plant container-grown perennials. Fertilize perennials as they start to grow. Weed and water as needed. Lay summer mulch in beds and borders. Deadhead faded flowers. Pinch back mums. Watch for pests and signs of disease.

Sow perennials and biennials for plants to bloom next year. Plant container-grown perennials. Fertilize perennials as they start to grow. Weed and water as needed. Lay summer mulch in beds and borders. Deadhead faded flowers unless you want plants to self-sow. Pinch back mums. Watch for pests and signs of disease.

Plant container-grown perennials. Weed and water as needed. Lay summer mulch in beds and borders. Deadhead faded flowers unless you want plants to self-sow. Pinch back mums. Watch for pests and signs of disease.

Weed and water as needed. Deadhead faded flowers unless you want plants to self-sow. Pinch back mums. Make notes on which plants will need division in fall. Check stakes on tall plants. Make notes for plants to order for fall planting to fill gaps in blooming season. Watch for pests and signs of disease.

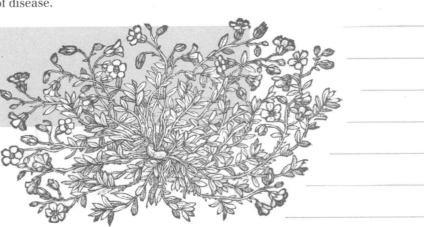

See Zone 8

See Zone 8

Bulbs

Annuals

1-3	Plant summer bulbs when soil is warm; put stakes in place for tall dahlias and gladiolus. Weed and water bulbs as necessary. Deadhead faded flowers of spring bulbs; leave foliage in place.	Plant out hardy annuals; plant out tender annuals when danger of frost is past. If late frost is likely, cover plants. Sprinkle any frosted plants with cool water before sun comes up; they may recover. Fertilize as plants begin to grow. Weed and water as needed. Watch for pests and signs of disease.
4	Plant summer bulbs when soil is warm; put stakes in place for tall dahlias and gladiolus. Make second planting of glads around mid–June for later bloom. Fertilize when six to eight inches tall. Weed and water bulbs as necessary. Deadhead faded flowers of spring bulbs; leave foliage in place.	Direct-sow or plant out tender annuals when danger of frost is past. Thin seedlings planted last month. Fertilize annuals as plants begin to grow, and when they start blooming. Weed and water as needed. Watch for pests and signs of disease.
5	Plant successions of gladiolus; plant other summer bulbs. Put stakes in place for tall dahlias, lilies, and gladiolus. Fertilize when six to eight inches tall. Weed and water bulbs as needed. Deadhead faded flowers of spring bulbs; remove foliage when it yellows and dries. Dig and divide crowded spring bulbs.	Direct-sow or plant out tender annuals. Fertilize new seedlings with liquid fertilizer, older plants as they begin to bloom. Thin seedlings planted earlier. Weed and water as needed. Deadhead faded flowers promptly. Watch for pests and signs of disease.
6	Plant successions of gladiolus; plant other summer bulbs. Put stakes in place for tall dahlias, lilies, and gladiolus. Fertilize when six to eight inches tall. Weed and water bulbs as needed. Deadhead faded flowers of spring bulbs; remove foliage when it yellows and dries. Dig, divide, and replant crowded spring bulbs. Watch for pests and signs of disease.	See Zone 5
7	Plant summer bulbs. Put stakes in place for tall dahlias, lilies, and gladiolus. Fertilize when six to eight inches tall. Weed and water bulbs as needed. Remove foliage of spring bulbs when it yellows and dries. Dig, divide, and replant crowded spring bulbs. Watch for pests and signs of disease.	See Zone 5
8	Plant summer bulbs. Fertilize as they grow. Place stakes for tall dahlias, lilies, and gladiolus. Weed, water as needed. Remove spring bulb foliage when it yellows and dries. Dig, divide, and replant crowded spring bulbs. Dig tulips and hyacinths after foliage yellows; discard bulbs or let dry in sun; remove dead leaves; store in cool, dry place to replant in fall. Watch for pests and disease.	Direct-sow tender annuals in bare spots, or set out new plants to replace fatigued plants. Feed new seedlings with liquid fertilizer, older plants regularly. Thin seedlings planted earlier. Weed and water as needed. Deadhead faded flowers promptly. Watch for pests and signs of disease.
9	Plant summer bulbs. Fertilize as plants begin to grow. Put stakes in place for tall dahlias, lilies, and gladiolus. Weed and water bulbs as needed. Remove foliage of spring bulbs when it yellows and dries. Dig, divide, and replant crowded spring bulbs. Watch for pests and signs of disease.	Continue planting tender annuals in bare spots and to replace fatigued plants. Remove spent plants from garden. Feed new seedlings with liquid fertilizer, older plants regularly. Thin seedlings planted earlier. Weed and water as needed. Be sure tall plants have stakes and annual vines are attached to supports. Deadhead faded flowers promptly. Watch for pests and signs of disease.
10-11	See Zone 9	See Zone 9

Container Gardens

Vegetables & Herbs

Plant cool-weather annuals and vegetables in containers. When danger of frost is past, plant tender annuals and herbs and summer vegetables. Move tender plants kept indoors for winter back outdoors when weather warms. Feed new plants with liquid fertilizer. Water containers as needed. Deadhead pansies. Watch for pests and signs of disease.	Plant out summer crops and herbs when soil warms. Mulch when plants are several inches high. Water as needed; store water where sun can warm it, and try to water at midday. Weed unmulched areas. Watch for pests and signs of disease.	*1-3*
When danger of frost is past, plant tender annuals and herbs and summer vegetables in containers. Move tender plants kept indoors for winter back outdoors when weather warms. Feed new plants with liquid fertilizer. Water containers as needed. Deadhead pansies. Watch for pests and signs of disease.	Harvest early crops. Set out summer vegetables and tender herbs when soil is warm. At end of month sow cabbage family in cold frame for fall crop. Thin seedlings sown earlier. Mulch when plants are several inches high. Weed, water, and fertilize as needed. Watch for pests and signs of disease.	*4*
Plant tender annuals and herbs and summer vegetables in containers. Move tender plants kept indoors for winter back outdoors when weather warms. Fertilize container plants regularly. Water as needed. Deadhead faded flowers. Watch for pests and signs of disease.	Harvest early crops. Set out last of summer vegetables and tender herbs. Plant successions of salad and root crops. At end of month, sow cabbage family in cold frame for fall crop. Thin seedlings sown earlier. Mulch when plants are several inches high. Have supports in place for peas and beans. Weed, water, and fertilize as needed. Watch for pests and signs of disease.	*5*
See Zone 5	See Zone 5	*6*
Move tender plants kept indoors for winter back outdoors when weather warms. Fertilize container plants regularly. Water as needed. Provide supports for climbing plants. Deadhead faded flowers. Watch for pests and signs of disease.	Harvest early crops. Early in month set out last of summer vegetables and tender herbs. Plant successions of root crops. Thin seedlings sown earlier. Mulch when plants are several inches high. Have supports in place for tall and climbing plants. Weed, water, and fertilize as needed. Pull spent crops. Turn compost pile. Watch for pests and signs of disease.	*7*
Fertilize container plants regularly. Water as needed. Provide supports for climbing plants. Deadhead faded flowers. Watch for pests and signs of disease.	Harvest early crops. Direct-sow warm-season crops for fall harvest. Thin seedlings sown earlier. Mulch when plants are several inches high. Check stakes and supports for tall and climbing plants. Weed, water, and fertilize as needed. Pull spent crops. Turn compost pile. Watch for pests and signs of disease.	*8*
See Zone 8	Harvest early crops. Sow warm-season crops indoors for fall harvest. Thin seedlings sown earlier. Mulch when plants are several inches high. Check stakes and supports for tall and climbing plants. Weed, water, and fertilize as needed. Pull spent crops. Turn compost pile. Watch for pests and signs of disease.	*9*
See Zone 8	See Zone 9	*10-11*

Fruit

1-3	Thin fruit on apples and pears when marble-sized. Water new plantings deeply if weather is dry. If late frost strikes, prune damaged new growth. Watch for signs of pests and disease. Trap larvae on tree trunks and destroy. Pick up dropped fruit and leaves.
4	Thin fruit on apples and pears when marble-sized. Remove raspberry suckers. Water deeply if weather is dry. Mulch blueberries. Watch for pests and signs of disease. Trap larvae on tree trunks and destroy. Pick up dropped fruit and leaves.
5	Thin tree fruit when marble-sized. Remove raspberry suckers. Water new plantings deeply if weather is dry. Mulch blueberries. Watch for pests and signs of disease. Trap larvae on tree trunks and destroy. Pick up dropped fruit and leaves.
6	Harvest strawberries when ripe. Cover ripening berries with netting to protect from birds. Thin tree fruit when marble-sized. Remove raspberry suckers. Water new plantings deeply if weather is dry. Mulch blueberries. Watch for pests and signs of disease. Trap larvae on tree trunks and destroy. Prune wood damaged by fire blight. Pick up dropped fruit and leaves.
7	Harvest ripe fruit. Cover ripening berries with netting to protect from birds. Cut raspberry canes back to ground after harvest. Water new plantings deeply if weather is dry. Watch for pests and signs of disease. Trap larvae on tree trunks and destroy. Prune wood damaged by fire blight. Pick up dropped fruit and leaves.
8	See Zone 7
9	Harvest ripe fruit. Cover ripening berries with netting to protect from birds. Cut brambles back to ground after harvest. Fertilize citrus and tropical fruit. Thin tree fruits. Water deeply if weather is dry. Watch for pests and signs of disease. Trap larvae on tree trunks. Prune wood damaged by fire blight. Pick up dropped fruit and leaves.
10-11	See Zone 9

Water-Saving Strategies

Water plants only when they need it, rather than on a preset schedule.

Water thoroughly, to a depth of at least two feet (deeper for deeper-rooted plants).

Water slowly to avoid runoff. If water does run off, stop immediately because you will know the soil is saturated.

Water at ground level, aiming directly at the root zone, rather than from overhead.

Water in the morning or late afternoon.

Recycle water from dehumidifiers, air conditioners, rain gutters. Learn how to safely recycle "gray water" from dishwashing, showers, and other household uses.

Collect water in an old-fashioned rain barrel for use in the garden.

Mulch the garden to slow the rate at which moisture evaporates from soil.

Do not water if rain is predicted.

Keep the garden weeded (weeds steal water from garden plants).

Remove spent plants promptly.

Grow drought-tolerant plants.

Set up windbreaks.

If watering is banned because of water shortage, prune trees to reduce their demand on root systems.

Do not overfertilize with nitrogen (causes excessive topgrowth).

July

Fighting Pests and Diseases

July is the height of the summer growing season, and it is also prime time for pests and diseases. This month we will look at some strategies for combatting these garden problems.

The best way to deal with pest and disease problems is to prevent them in the first place. This is not as simplistic as it sounds; the way you care for your plants really does have some effect on the amount and severity of disease and pest infestation they are likely to suffer.

Of primary importance is simply keeping the garden clean. Deadhead faded flowers regularly; pick up fallen leaves and dropped fruit. Plant debris offers sites for disease organisms to grow, and places for insects to lay eggs and overwinter. Once disease organisms are present you may unknowingly spread them from plant to plant in the course of your normal gardening activities. To decrease the risk, do not work around plants when they are wet. If you are a smoker, do not smoke in the garden, especially around members of the nightshade family (tomatoes, eggplant, and petunias, for example). Wash your hands before working in the garden.

If you have to prune diseased growth from plants, sterilize the tools you use *after every cut*. Dip the tools in rubbing alcohol or a solution of one part liquid chlorine bleach to nine parts water.

Sound cultural practices produce sturdy, vigorous plants that are better able to withstand attacks by pests and disease when they do occur. Build good soil for the plants to grow in. Make sure plants receive an adequate supply of nutrients, but do not overfeed them. Water when plants need it, but do not overwater—both drought and oversaturation weaken plants.

When possible, grow varieties that are resistant to or at least tolerant of pests and diseases that are common in your area, or that seem to plague your garden year after year.

If you grow vegetables, rotate susceptible crops through the garden, planting them in a different location each year to prevent buildups of soilborne pathogens and overwintering pest populations. In particular, do not plant members of the same botanical family in the same part of the vegetable garden year after year. Brassicas (plants in the cabbage family), for example, are prone to clubroot and other diseases that build up in the soil over time.

Monitor your plants carefully throughout the year, and act promptly when you notice the first symptoms of pests and diseases. The problem will only get worse the longer you let it go untreated.

When pest problems do occur, as they inevitably will, the smartest way to fight them is to try the least severe control measures first. Don't just pick up a can of the strongest insecticide you can find and blast away—for the good of the environment, such products should be used only when they are absolutely necessary, not as a panacea. The gentler the measures you take, the less chance there will be that you may harm the birds, bees, butterflies, and other beneficial creatures that share your garden, or your pets, your kids, or even yourself. Save the strong stuff until you really need it.

One type of pest control is to employ what is called mechanical controls. Cover fruit trees and bushes with special netting to keep birds away from ripening fruit. Floating row covers made of spun-bonded polyester or polypropylene keep pests off of plants while letting in light, air, and water. They are also helpful early and late in the growing season when unseasonable light frosts occur. Cardboard collars placed around young seedlings will keep cutworms from gnawing through the delicate stems. Effective lures and traps are available for a number of pests, as well. Sticky yellow traps are excellent whitefly controls. There are also red traps for codling moths and traps baited with pheromone lures for Japanese beetles. Crawling insects that lay their eggs on the trunks of trees can be trapped with Tanglefoot, the sticky substance that coats old-fashioned flypaper. To trap the larvae you can wrap burlap around the tree trunks, securing it at the top and bottom, and periodically remove and dispose of it, pests and all. If slugs are the bane of your garden, you can trap them in pans of stale beer sunk into the ground, or go out after dark with a flashlight and sprinkle them with salt when you find them. The most time-honored means of mechanical control is simple handpicking. If the invaders are big enough to grab, put on a pair of gloves and pick them off your plants. Crush the bugs or drop them into a can containing some water and a bit of kerosene.

Biological control involves releasing into the garden predatory insects that will eat the pests or interfere with their reproductive cycles. If you notice ladybugs or green lacewings in your garden, some biological control is already going on. Learn to recognize these and other beneficial insects so you don't kill them by mistake. Biological controls are available by mail from a number of companies. See the Appendixes, page 89.

Insecticidal soap provides an excellent, nontoxic means of control for small insects such as aphids, mites, and whiteflies. Spray it directly onto the pests, and

repeat daily until they are gone. Handle the product with care, as you would any pest control material, and follow the directions on the package.

Horticultural or dormant oil sprays (so called because they are applied in late winter, when plants are dormant) can be used to control numerous pests, including scale and mealybugs, on fruit-bearing and ornamental trees. The oil suffocates overwintering pests, eggs, and larvae.

A means of handling caterpillars, slugs, and other soft-bodied pests is to sprinkle wood ashes or diatomaceous earth around the perimeter of the garden or around prized plants. Both substances contain sharp-edged particles which damage the membranes covering the pests. Reapply after rain.

Botanical (plant-derived) poisons and chemical dusts and sprays should be the weapons of last resort. Botanical insecticides include pyrethrum, ryania, sabadilla, neem, and nicotine. Their advantage over so-called chemical products is that they break down more quickly upon exposure to light, air, and water, and do not remain in the environment for long. Whether you use botanical or chemical insecticides, it is imperative that you use them with great caution. Handle them carefully, always wearing gloves, and follow explicitly the package directions for application and use. Store the containers properly, and keep them away from children and pets. Finally, dispose of any unused products correctly—they are hazardous household wastes and should not simply be tossed in the trash or flushed down the toilet. Contact local government officials if you don't know the proper disposal procedures in your area.

Disease problems are more difficult to fight than pests, especially for organic gardeners. The first line of defense is prevention: practicing good garden hygiene, sound cultural techniques, and crop rotation in the vegetable garden. There are some sulfur-based fungicides on the market that can be effective. Sometimes prompt removal of diseased plant parts can keep the affliction from spreading. Pinch off mildewed leaves; prune damaged tree branches back to healthy wood. If the problem persists, the only remedy for organic gardeners is to remove the affected plant and hope the infection hasn't spread to its neighbors.

There is, of course, an arsenal of chemical fungicides available; spotless roses, unblemished fruit, and perfect lawns are probably the most difficult garden goals to achieve without their use, although it is possible to grow all three organically. If you do use these products, handle them with care and follow the package directions to the letter.

Water new plantings deeply during dry weather. Water established trees and shrubs in very dry years. Fertilize established trees and shrubs, but no later than July, so new growth can harden before cold weather. Take softwood cuttings.

See Zone 3

Order stock for fall planting. Plant container-grown stock if weather is not too hot. Water new plantings deeply. Water established trees and shrubs in dry weather. Fertilize established trees, shrubs, and broad-leaved evergreens again. Trim hedges. Take softwood cuttings. Watch for pests and signs of disease.

See Zone 5

Order stock for fall planting. Water new plantings deeply. Water established trees and shrubs in dry weather. Fertilize established trees, shrubs, and broad-leaved evergreens again. Prune summer-blooming shrubs and vines when finished flowering. Trim hedges. Take softwood cuttings. Watch for pests and signs of disease.

Order stock for fall planting. Water new plantings deeply. Water established trees and shrubs in dry weather. Prune summer-blooming shrubs and vines when they finish flowering. Trim hedges. Take softwood cuttings. Watch for pests and signs of disease.

Water deeply new plantings, established trees, and shrubs in dry weather; water early or late in day. Prune summer-blooming shrubs and vines when they finish flowering. Trim hedges. Take softwood cuttings. Watch for pests and signs of disease.

See Zone 9

Fertilize roses for last time six weeks before you expect first frost. Water if weather is dry. Deadhead faded flowers. Watch for pests and signs of disease.	Mow lawn at high mower setting in summer. Water lawn and ground covers when necessary.	*1-3*
See Zone 3	See Zone 3	*4*
Fertilize roses. Water if weather is dry. Deadhead faded flowers. Prune climbers and ramblers when they finish blooming. Watch for pests and signs of disease.	Order ground covers and ornamental grasses for fall planting. Plant container-grown grasses and ground covers. Mow lawn at high mower setting in summer. Water grasses and ground covers when necessary. Take cuttings of ground covers to start new plants.	*5*
Order roses for fall planting. Fertilize roses. Water if weather is dry. Deadhead faded flowers. Prune climbers and ramblers when they finish blooming. Watch for pests and signs of disease.	See Zone 5	*6*
Order roses for fall planting. Fertilize roses. Water if weather is dry. Deadhead faded flowers. Prune climbers and ramblers when they finish flowering. Watch for pests and signs of disease. Keep fallen leaves picked up to prevent black spot.	See Zone 5	*7*
See Zone 7	Order ground covers and ornamental grasses for fall planting. Plant warm-season lawn grasses. Fertilize and water new lawns. Water established grasses and ground covers when necessary. Mow lawn at high mower setting. Take cuttings of ground covers to start new plants.	*8*
Order roses for fall planting. Fertilize roses. Water if weather is dry. Watch for pests and signs of disease. Keep fallen leaves cleaned up to prevent black spot.	Water grasses and ground covers when necessary. Mow lawn at high mower setting. Take cuttings of ground covers to start new plants.	*9*
See Zone 9	See Zone 9	*10-11*

Zone	Perennials	Bulbs
1-3	Sow perennials and biennials in cold frame for plants to bloom next year. Weed, water, and fertilize as necessary. Deadhead faded flowers. Watch for pests and signs of disease. Divide crowded plants when finished blooming.	Order hardy bulbs for fall planting. Fertilize summer bulbs. Water during dry weather. Deadhead faded flowers.
4	See Zone 3	Fertilize summer bulbs. Water during dry weather. Make sure tall lilies, dahlias, and glads have stakes. Deadhead faded flowers.
5	Order perennials for fall planting. Sow perennials and biennials for plants to bloom next year. Plant container-grown perennials. Weed, water, and fertilize as necessary. Deadhead faded flowers. Finish pinching mums by mid-month. Make sure tall plants have stakes. Watch for pests and signs of disease.	Order bulbs for fall planting. Fertilize summer bulbs. Make sure tall lilies, dahlias, and glads have stakes. Water during dry weather. Dig and divide crowded bulbs.
6	Order perennials for fall planting. Sow perennials and biennials for plants to bloom next year. Plant container-grown perennials. Weed, water, and fertilize as necessary. Deadhead faded flowers. Pinch mums for last time. Make sure tall plants have stakes. Watch for pests and signs of disease.	See Zone 5
7	Order perennials for fall planting. Remove spent biennials; replace with annuals. Weed, water, and fertilize as necessary. Deadhead faded flowers unless you want plants to self-sow. Pinch mums for last tlme. Make sure tall plants have stakes. Mulch gardens for hottest part of summer. Watch for pests and signs of disease.	See Zone 5
8	Order perennials for fall planting. Remove spent biennials; replace with annuals. Plant container-grown fall bloomers, give the plants some shade until established. Weed, water, and fertilize as necessary. Deadhead faded flowers unless you want plants to self-sow. Pinch mums for last time. Stake tall plants. Mulch beds and borders for hottest part of summer. Watch for pests and disease.	Order spring bulbs for fall planting. Fertilize summer bulbs. Make sure tall lilies, dahlias, and glads have stakes. Water during dry weather.
9	Weed, water, and fertilize as necessary. Deadhead faded flowers; cut back ragged-looking plants and brown ferns to stimulate new growth. Pinch mums. Keep beds and borders well mulched through hottest part of summer. Watch for pests and signs of disease.	Water during dry weather. Deadhead summer bulbs as they finish blooming.
10-11	See Zone 9	See Zone 9

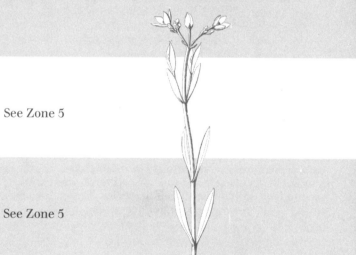

Annuals

Weed, water, and fertilize as needed. Deadhead faded flowers. Watch for pests and signs of disease.

Sow pansies for fall flowers. Weed, water, and fertilize as needed. Deadhead faded flowers. Watch for pests and signs of disease.

Sow pansies for fall flowers. Weed, water, and fertilize as needed. Deadhead faded flowers. Cut back or replace worn-out plants. Take cuttings to pot up for winter house-plants. Watch for pests and signs of disease.

See Zone 5

See Zone 5

Set out new plants in bare spaces. Weed, water, and fertilize as needed. Deadhead faded flowers. Mulch beds and borders through hottest part of summer. Cut back or replace worn-out plants. Watch for pests and signs of disease.

See Zone 8

See Zone 8

Zone	Container Gardens	Vegetables & Herbs
1-3	Harvest vegetables and herbs, cut flowers from container gardens. Weed and fertilize container plants regularly. Water as often as needed. Deadhead faded flowers. Watch for pests and signs of disease.	Harvest vegetables and herbs. Weed, water, and fertilize as needed. Remove spent plants. Turn compost pile. Check supports on tall and climbing plants. Watch for pests and signs of disease.
4	See Zone 3	Harvest vegetables and herbs. Direct-sow cool-weather crops for fall harvest. Weed, water, and fertilize as needed. Remove spent plants. Turn compost pile. Check supports on tall and climbing plants. Watch for pests and signs of disease.
5	See Zone 3	Keep up with harvest. Direct-sow cool-weather crops for fall harvest. Transplant cabbage family seedlings to garden. Weed, water, and fertilize as needed. Remove spent plants. Turn compost pile. Check supports on tall and climbing plants. Watch for pests and signs of disease.
6	See Zone 3	Keep up with harvest. Late in month, direct-sow cool-weather crops for fall harvest. Transplant cabbage family seedlings to garden. Weed, water, and fertilize as needed. Remove spent plants. Turn compost pile. Check supports on tall and climbing plants. Watch for pests and signs of disease.
7	See Zone 3	Keep up with harvest; pick leafy greens in morning. Direct-sow cool-weather crops for fall harvest. Transplant cabbage family seedlings to garden. Weed, water, and fertilize as needed. Mulch or give afternoon shade to leafy crops. Let dill, coriander, fennel self-sow. Remove spent plants. Turn compost pile. Check supports on tall and climbing plants. Watch for pests and disease.
8	See Zone 3	Keep up with harvest. Sow cabbage family for fall harvest. Plant out new tomatoes. Weed, water, fertilize as needed. Be sure garden is well mulched for hottest part of summer. Give afternoon shade to leafy crops. Cut back bushy herbs. Take cuttings of perennial herbs to start new plants. Remove spent plants. Turn compost pile. Check supports on tall and climbing plants. Watch for pests and disease.
9	Harvest vegetables and herbs, cut flowers from container gardens. Weed and fertilize regularly. Water as often as needed. Deadhead faded flowers. Watch for pests and signs of disease.	Keep up with harvest. Sow cool-season crops indoors for fall planting. Plant out new tomatoes. Weed, water, and fertilize as needed. Be sure garden is well mulched for hottest part of summer. Cut back bushy herbs. Take cuttings of perennial herbs to start new plants. Remove spent plants. Turn compost pile. Check supports on tall and climbing plants. Watch for pests and signs of disease.
10-11	See Zone 9	See Zone 9

Fruit

Harvest ripe fruit. Cover ripening berries with netting to protect them from birds. Prune brambles after harvest. Water during dry spells. Watch for pests and signs of disease.

Harvest ripe fruit. Cover ripening berries with netting to protect them from birds. Prune brambles after harvest. Fertilize strawberries after harvest or top-dress with compost. Water during dry spells. Layer brambles to start new plants (see page 58). Watch for pests and signs of disease.

Harvest ripe fruit. Fertilize strawberries after harvest or top-dress with compost. Remove all but three to four fruits on melon plants for best quality. Prune early-bearing raspberries when harvest is over; cut out suckers. Mulch brambles; water deeply if weather is dry. Layer brambles to start new plants. Watch for pests and signs of disease.

Order stock for fall planting. Harvest ripe fruit. Fertilize strawberries after harvest or top-dress with compost. Thin fruit on heavy-bearing trees. Cut back raspberries after harvest; cut out suckers. Water spring-planted stock in dry weather. Pick up dropped fruit daily. Cover ripening berries with netting to keep away birds. Watch for pests and signs of disease.

Order stock for fall planting. Harvest ripe fruit. Thin fruit on heavy-bearing trees. Water spring-planted stock in dry weather. Pick up dropped fruit daily. Cover ripening fruit with netting to keep away birds. Watch for pests and signs of disease.

Order stock for fall planting. Harvest ripe fruit. Thin fruit on heavy-bearing trees. Water deeply in dry weather. Pick up dropped fruit daily. Cut back brambles after harvest. Prune out suckers around base of trees. Watch for pests and signs of disease.

Order stock for fall planting. Harvest ripe fruit. Thin fruit on heavy-bearing trees. Water deeply in dry weather. Pick up dropped fruit daily. Cut back brambles after harvest. Prune citrus. Prune suckers around base of trees. Watch for pests and signs of disease.

See Zone 9

Coping with Four-Footed Pests

Mice, voles, and rabbits love to hide in the mulch around tender-barked trees in winter, and nibble at the bark. To discourage them, mulch in a ring extending from the tree's drip line to eight to twelve inches from the trunk; this is the area where most of the roots are concentrated. For winter protection, install a mouse guard—surround the trunk with a cylinder of hardware cloth or vinyl tree wrap. Or wrap the trunk with tree-wrap paper from the ground to just below the lowest branches.

If mice gnaw on your bulbs, you can plant daffodils and narcissus, which they don't like, instead of tulips, which they do. Or, excavate the soil from the bulb bed, line the bed with hardware cloth, then replace the soil and replant the bulbs.

The best—although not the most aesthetically pleasing—way to keep rabbits out of the garden is to surround it with a sturdy fence of chicken wire or hardware cloth that is two and a half feet tall and extends six inches underground.

Deer are the worst problem for many gardeners, and there are multitudes of tactics for keeping them out of the garden. None of them, unfortunately, are foolproof. Basically, if deer are hungry enough they will eat just about anything, and plants they would normally avoid will be on the menu along with the rest. Deer can easily leap an eight-foot fence; you could put up a very high fence, and angle the top edge inward for a couple of feet. Or try laying hardware cloth or chicken wire on the ground; deer are said not to like walking on the wire.

Various repellents are on the market, which have varying degrees of success for different gardens at different times. You can also try hanging bags of human hair or bars of deodorant soap around the garden, or sprinkling dried blood around the plants.

One persistent rumor where I live is that placing a salt lick on another part of the property will lure deer away from the garden.

Probably the only sure cure is to put up a greenhouse and do your gardening there!

August

Gardening in Containers

The world of container gardening is not limited to pots of geraniums and pansies. You can grow a dwarf evergreen in a container, or a rosebush, or a genetic dwarf fruit tree. Herbs, vegetables, vines, perennials, annuals—all sorts of plants will grow happily in containers of adequate size.

Containers are a great way to garden, whether you use them as an adjunct to beds and borders in the ground or as gardens in themselves. Containers expand your garden possibilities. You can grow plants in places where a conventional garden would be impossible—such as on a patio or city rooftop—and you can also grow plants that are not hardy in your part of the country, by simply moving the pots indoors in winter. In a container you can grow a plant that needs special care or a different type of soil from what's available in your garden.

A pretty pot will show off a favorite plant and make it look really special. A big, bold plant in a pot creates a dramatic focal point.

For a gardenlike effect in a small space, you can group lots of potted plants together. Use plants of different heights and sizes to create a feeling of depth, or set the pots on shelves or tiered stands to put the plants at different heights.

Potted plants add their own kind of charm to the house and grounds. Windowboxes overflowing with flowers lend a romantic air to a house, and soften the look of an otherwise severe facade. Containers of plants grouped by the front door or along the steps welcome visitors to your home. Hanging baskets suspended from the ceiling of a porch create a shady retreat for a hot summer day. Tall potted plants can be placed below the hanging baskets to make a leafy privacy screen.

On a deck, patio, or rooftop, or even in the backyard, plants in containers can be useful as well as attractive. A row of large tubs holding trellised vines or tall flowering plants or shrubs can be used to create privacy, divide space, or screen off an undesirable view. And if you change your mind halfway through the season, all you need to do is move the containers to remove the screen or change its configuration.

There are many sorts of containers available for plants. Traditional clay flowerpots come in a host of different sizes, and there are also other terra cotta containers, both plain and decorated, in an array of shapes and sizes—boxes, bowls, vases, windowbox shapes, strawberry jars, urns, and tubs. Clay pots allow air through their porous walls, and their earthy color harmonizes nicely with most flower colors and all shades of greenery. One drawback to clay pots is that moisture evaporates through those porous walls, which can be a problem in summer, and large clay containers are quite heavy when filled with soil.

Plastic is the material of choice for many gardeners. Plastic containers are lightweight and hold moisture well (sometimes too well), and come in a variety of colors. White, dark green, and brown are most popular, and there are also terra cotta–colored plastic pots that mimic the look of clay but are lighter in weight. Plastic pots come in many shapes and sizes. The weight advantage makes plastic the most widely used material for hanging baskets.

If you like the convenience of simple clay or plastic pots but want a more decorative look, set the pot inside a decorative cachepot of glazed ceramic, porcelain, stone, metal, or wood. If the decorative container has no drainage hole in the bottom, set the inner pot on a layer of pebbles so the pot will not sit in runoff water. Or you can simply check the pots after a rain or watering and pour off any excess water.

Another widely used material for containers, especially large ones, is wood. Wooden windowboxes, rectangular and square planter boxes, tubs, barrels, and half-barrels have an appealing country style, and their neutral gray-brown color is a fine ground against which to display flowers of any hue.

Planting Containers

When you garden in containers you can give plants the perfect soil mix. A good potting medium is loose-textured, porous, and well-aerated, and drains well while still retaining enough moisture for plants. Potting media are lighter in texture than most garden soils, but they must have enough body to support the plants.

You can purchase preblended potting mixtures or create your own. The packaged soilless mixes are peat-based, and can be used right out of the bag (after moistening). But I find that for outdoor growing I prefer to add some soil to this kind of mix to give it more substance. I like to add some crumbled compost or leaf mold as well.

You can also create your own custom-blended potting media. A good potting mix needs a lightening agent to give it porosity (vermiculite, perlite, or sharp builder's sand), organic matter, (compost, leaf mold, peat moss, or composted manure), and additional nutrients from synthetic or natural fertilizers. Whether or not the medium contains soil is a matter of personal preference.

Caring for Potted Plants

Plants growing in containers are almost entirely dependent on you, the gardener, for the water and nutrients

they need in order to grow. You will need to water and fertilize potted plants more often than plants growing in beds and borders in the ground.

Container plants dry out quickly outdoors, especially in hot, dry, windy weather, because the small volume of soil in a container cannot hold its moisture for long. You will probably need to water plants in all containers smaller than tubs, barrels, and large planter boxes every day in order to give plants the moisture essential to their growth. Small pots may need watering more than once a day. Grouping potted plants together slows evaporation, and moisture evaporates more slowly from plastic pots than from porous clay.

Check container plants every day in summer, and give them as much water as they need, whenever the potting mix feels dry to the touch immediately below the soil surface.

Water thoroughly, until the excess runs out the drainage holes in the bottom of the pot. Thorough watering is important to saturate the root ball fully, and also to flush excess fertilizer salts from the pot. These salts could eventually harm plants if allowed to accumulate.

If you spend many hours away from home, you may want to invest in an automatic watering system for your container garden. Scaled-down versions of drip irrigation systems, designed specially for use in containers, are widely available.

Fertilize container plants often. Liquid fertilizers are generally easiest to use. Organic gardeners can use fish emulsion, seaweed concentrate, or manure "tea." Others can choose among an array of liquid and granular products that are dissolved in water for use. Follow package directions when mixing fertilizer solutions. Don't make them stronger than recommended; overfeeding pushes plants to grow too fast, and the resulting weak growth is highly susceptible to pest and disease damage.

Follow package directions regarding frequency of use, as well. Generally speaking, you can fertilize container annuals, perennials, vegetables, and herbs every couple of weeks; roses, shrubs, and trees once a month. Keep an eye on your plants—if they look healthy, you're probably fertilizing them correctly.

Plant evergreens. Make sure spring-planted stock gets water in dry weather. Pinch off soft new growth in late summer to help plants harden for winter. Take softwood cuttings of shrubs. Watch for pests and signs of disease. **1-3**

See Zone 3 **4**

Order stock for fall planting. Plant container-grown evergreens if weather is not too stressful. Make sure spring-planted stock gets water in hot, dry weather. Trim hedges. Prune summer-blooming vines and shrubs after they finish flowering. Take softwood cuttings. Watch for pests and signs of disease. **5**

Order stock for fall planting. Plant container-grown evergreens if weather is not too stressful. Make sure spring-planted stock gets water in hot, dry weather; water established plants during extended dry spells. Trim hedges. Prune summer-blooming vines and shrubs after they finish flowering. Take softwood cuttings. Watch for pests and signs of disease. **6**

Order stock for fall planting. Plant container-grown evergreens if weather is not too stressful. Make sure new plants get water in hot, dry weather; water established plants during extended dry spells. Trim hedges, topiaries, and espaliers. Prune summer-blooming shrubs and vines after they finish flowering. Take softwood cuttings. Watch for pests and signs of disease. **7**

Order stock for fall planting. Make sure new plantings get plenty of water; water established plants as needed. Lay fresh mulch around shrubs. Trim hedges, topiaries, and espaliers. Prune water sprouts and suckers from young trees. Prune summer-blooming shrubs and vines when they finish flowering. Take softwood cuttings. Watch for pests and signs of disease. **8**

Order stock for fall planting. Plant palms and tropical plants. Make sure new plantings get plenty of water; water established plants as needed. Fertilize spring bloomers now setting buds. Lay fresh mulch around shrubs. Trim hedges, topiaries, and espaliers. Prune water sprouts and suckers from young trees. Take softwood cuttings. Watch for pests and signs of disease. **9**

See Zone 9 **10-11**

1-3

Deadhead faded flowers. Clip off new growth in late summer to help plants harden. Water if weather is dry. Watch for pests and signs of disease. Around end of month, mound soil around base of plants for winter protection.

Reseed bare or thin spots in lawn; seed new lawns by mid-August so grass can get established before cold weather. Fertilize established lawns late August or early September. Water if weather is dry; water new plantings regularly.

4

Deadhead faded flowers. Clip off new growth in late summer to help plants harden. Water if weather is dry. Take softwood cuttings of shrub roses to start new plants. Around end of month, mound soil around base of plants for winter protection. Watch for pests and signs of disease.

See Zone 3

5

Fertilize for last time six weeks before you expect first fall frost. Deadhead faded flowers. Water if weather is dry. Take softwood cuttings of shrub roses to start new plants. Watch for pests and signs of disease.

Reseed bare or thin spots in lawn; seed new lawns mid to late August so grass can get established before cold weather. Fertilize established lawns or top-dress with compost. Aerate and de-thatch if necessary. Water new lawns regularly, established lawns if weather is dry. Mow weekly. Take cuttings of ground covers to start new plants.

6

Order roses for fall planting. Fertilize for last time six weeks before you expect first fall frost. Deadhead faded flowers. Water if weather is dry. Take softwood cuttings of shrub roses to start new plants. Pick up dropped leaves. Watch for pests and signs of disease.

Order ornamental grasses for fall planting. Water lawns as needed in dry weather. Mow weekly. Weed ground cover areas if necessary.

7

See Zone 6

See Zone 6

8

Order roses for fall planting. Fertilize. Deadhead faded flowers. Water as needed. Lay fresh mulch, or keep roses weeded. Pick up dropped leaves. Take softwood cuttings of shrub roses to start new plants. Watch for pests and signs of disease.

See Zone 6

9

Order roses for fall planting. Fertilize. Deadhead faded flowers. Water as needed. Lay fresh mulch, or keep roses weeded. Pick up dropped leaves. Watch for pests and signs of disease.

Order ornamental grasses for fall planting. Lay sod for warm-season lawns. Water lawns as needed in dry weather. Mow weekly. Weed ground cover areas if necessary.

10-11

See Zone 9

See Zone 9

Weed, water, and fertilize as necessary. Deadhead faded flowers. Watch for pests and signs of disease.

See Zone 3

At end of month, plant container-grown mums for fall flowers. Sow perennials and biennials for bloom next year. Weed, water, and fertilize as necessary. Deadhead faded flowers. Cut back early bloomers when foliage begins to die back. Divide crowded spring bloomers. Take cuttings to start new plants. Watch for pests and signs of disease. Prepare soil for fall planting.

Order stock for fall planting. Sow perennials and biennials for bloom next year. Weed, water, and fertilize as necessary. Deadhead faded flowers. Cut back early bloomers when foliage begins to die back. Divide crowded spring bloomers. Take cuttings to start new plants. Watch for pests and signs of disease. Prepare soil for fall planting.

Order stock for fall planting. Sow perennials and biennials for bloom next year. Weed, water, and fertilize as necessary. Deadhead faded flowers. Cut back early bloomers when foliage begins to die back. Divide crowded spring bloomers. Take cuttings to start new plants. Watch for pests and signs of disease.

Order stock for fall planting. Sow perennials and biennials for bloom next year. Weed, water, and fertilize as necessary. Deadhead faded flowers. Cut back early bloomers when foliage begins to die back. Lay fresh mulch where needed. Divide crowded spring bloomers. Take cuttings to start new plants. Watch for pests and signs of disease.

Order stock for fall planting. Weed, water, and fertilize as necessary. Deadhead faded flowers. Cut back early bloomers as foliage begins to die back. Lay fresh mulch in beds and borders. Divide crowded spring bloomers. Take cuttings to start new plants. Watch for pests and signs of disease.

See Zone 9

Bulbs

Annuals

Zone	Bulbs	Annuals
1-3	Order hardy bulbs for fall planting. Fertilize summer bulbs. Water during dry weather. Deadhead faded flowers. Cut lily stalks back to ground when they begin to die back. Watch for pests and signs of disease.	Weed, water, and fertilize as needed. Deadhead faded flowers. Watch for pests and signs of disease.
4	Order hardy bulbs for fall planting. Plant lily bulbs for bloom next year. Cut lilies back to ground when stalks die back. Water during dry weather. Fertilize summer bulbs. Deadhead faded flowers. Watch for pests and signs of disease.	See Zone 3
5	Order hardy bulbs for fall planting. Plant autumn crocus and colchicum for fall bloom. Water in dry weather. Fertilize summer bulbs. Deadhead faded flowers. Stake tall glads and dahlias. Cut lilies back to ground when stalks die back. Watch for pests and signs of disease.	Weed, water, and fertilize as needed. Deadhead faded flowers. Shear back smaller plants to promote fall reblooming. Watch for pests and signs of disease.
6	Order hardy bulbs for fall planting. Plant autumn crocus and colchicum. Water in dry weather. Fertilize summer bulbs. Deadhead faded flowers. Stake tall glads and dahlias. Cut lilies back to ground when stalks die back. Watch for pests and signs of disease.	See Zone 5
7	See Zone 6	Weed, water, and fertilize as needed. Deadhead faded flowers. Shear back plants whose blooms are slowing, to promote reblooming, or remove and replace with new plants. Remove mildewed and worn-out plants; do not compost mildewed plants. Watch for pests and signs of disease.
8	Order hardy bulbs for fall planting; store in refrigerator until planting time. Plant bulbs for late bloom: colchicum, sternbergia, lycoris. Water in dry weather. Fertilize summer bulbs. Deadhead faded flowers. Stake tall glads and dahlias. Cut lilies back to ground when stalks die back. Watch for pests and signs of disease.	Sow pansies indoors to plant out in October. Weed, water, and fertilize as needed. Lay fresh mulch on beds and borders. Deadhead faded flowers. Shear back plants whose blooms are slowing, to promote reblooming, or remove and replace with new plants. Remove worn-out plants. Watch for pests and disease. Remove but do not compost mildewed plants. Prepare soil for fall planting.
9	Order hardy bulbs for fall planting; store in refrigerator until planting time. Plant bulbs for late bloom: nerine, lycoris. Water bulbs in dry weather. Fertilize summer bulbs. Deadhead faded flowers. Stake tall glads and dahlias. Watch for pests and signs of disease.	Sow pansies and hardy annuals indoors to plant out in fall. Weed, water, and fertilize as needed. Lay fresh mulch on beds and borders. Deadhead faded flowers or shear back plants to promote reblooming. Remove and replace worn-out plants. Watch for pests and signs of disease. Remove but do not compost mildewed plants. Prepare soil for fall planting.
10-11	See Zone 9	Sow hardy annuals indoors to plant out in fall. Weed, water, and fertilize as needed. Lay fresh mulch on beds and borders. Deadhead faded flowers or shear back plants to promote reblooming. Remove and replace worn-out plants. Watch for pests and signs of disease. Remove but do not compost mildewed plants. Prepare soil for fall planting.

Container Gardens	Vegetables & Herbs	
Harvest vegetables and herbs, cut flowers from containers. Weed and fertilize plants regularly. Water as needed. Deadhead faded flowers. Watch for pests and signs of disease.	Keep up with harvest. Collect herb seeds when ripe. Disbud and prune tomatoes and squash to speed ripening of fruit. Weed, water, and fertilize as needed. Remove spent plants. Turn compost pile. Check supports on climbing plants. Watch for pests and signs of disease.	*1-3*
Harvest vegetables and herbs, cut flowers from containers. Weed and fertilize plants regularly. Water as needed. Deadhead faded flowers. Train climbers; trim and train topiaries. Watch for pests and signs of disease.	Keep up with harvest. Collect herb seeds when ripe. Remove buds and flowers from tomatoes and squash to speed ripening of fruit. Weed, water, and fertilize as needed. Thin seedlings sown last month. Remove spent plants. Sow cover crops in empty beds. Turn compost pile. Check supports on climbing plants. Watch for pests and signs of disease.	*4*
See Zone 4	Keep up with harvest. Collect herb seeds when ripe. Cut herbs to freeze and dry. Sow cool-weather crops in cold frame. Thin seedlings sown last month. Weed, water, and fertilize as needed. Remove spent plants. Sow cover crops in empty beds. Turn compost pile. Check supports on climbing plants. Take cuttings of perennial herbs to start new plants. Watch for pests and signs of disease.	*5*
See Zone 4	See Zone 5	*6*
See Zone 4	Keep up with harvest; cut herbs to dry and freeze. Direct-sow cool-weather crops. Plant out seedlings started indoors; shade plants until established. Weed, water, and fertilize as needed. Remove spent plants. Sow cover crops in empty beds. Turn compost pile. Check supports on climbing plants. Take cuttings of perennial herbs to start new plants. Watch for pests and disease.	*7*
Harvest vegetables and herbs, cut flowers from containers. Remove worn-out plants and replace with new ones. Weed and fertilize regularly. Water as needed. Deadhead faded flowers. Train climbers; trim and train topiaries. Watch for pests and signs of disease.	Keep up with harvest; cut herbs to dry and freeze. Sow cool-weather crops in garden or indoors. Weed, water, and fertilize as needed. Lay fresh mulch in garden. Remove spent plants. Turn compost pile. Check supports on climbing plants. Take cuttings of perennial herbs to start new plants. Watch for pests and signs of disease.	*8*
See Zone 8	Keep up with harvest; cut herbs to dry or freeze. Sow cool-weather crops indoors. Weed, water, and fertilize garden as needed. Lay fresh mulch. Remove spent plants. Turn compost pile. Check supports on climbing plants. Take cuttings of perennial herbs to start new plants. Watch for pests and signs of disease.	*9*
See Zone 8	See Zone 9	*10-11*

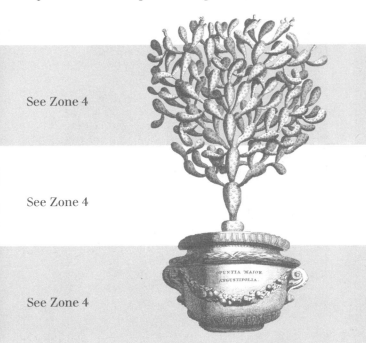

OPUNTIA MAIOR ANGUSTIFOLIA

1-3
Harvest ripe fruit. Fertilize strawberries. Replace thin mulches. Water during dry spells. Watch for pests and signs of disease.

4
Harvest ripe fruit. Fertilize strawberries; plant out runners rooted in pots. Replace thin mulches. Water during dry spells. Pick up dropped fruit. Watch for pests and signs of disease.

5
See Zone 4

6
Harvest ripe fruit. Plant out strawberry runners rooted in pots. Keep blueberries evenly moist; water other plants during dry spells. Replace thin mulches. Cut back old brambles when plants finish bearing. Pick up dropped fruit. Watch for pests and signs of disease.

7
See Zone 6

8
Harvest ripe fruit. Water deeply during dry weather. Lay fresh mulch. Cut back old brambles when plants finish bearing. Pick up dropped fruit. Watch for pests and signs of disease.

9
Harvest ripe fruit. Fertilize berries or top-dress with compost. Water deeply during dry weather. Lay fresh mulch. Cut back old brambles when plants finish bearing. Pick up dropped fruit. Watch for pests and signs of disease.

10-11
See Zone 9

How to Plant a Tub Garden

Here's how to plant a romantic, luxuriant garden in a single large container. A half-barrel is ideal, but you can use the same basic approach to fill a rectangular planter box, a square box, or a large pot.

To get the lush look you're after, you will need plants of three or four different sizes. If the tub or planter will be against a wall and viewed primarily from one side, place the tallest plants in the back of the container and low, trailing plants along the front edge. If the container will be seen from all sides, the tallest plants go in the center, and the low trailing plants all around the outer edge.

Fill the planter to within one to two inches of the top with moist potting mix. Plant the tallest plants first. You might choose a spiky dracaena for the vertical line of its leaves, or a clump of tall geraniums, blue salvia, or coreopsis. Work toward the front or outside of the container, setting plants of decreasing height. When the tall plants are in place, next plant medium-height plants in front of or surrounding the tall ones. Nicotiana or marguerite daisies would be good choices, as would silver-leaved dusty miller. In the front of the container, or around the edges, plant small edging plants, such as sweet alyssum, lobelia, or torenia. At intervals, set variegated vinca, ivy, or other trailing plants to cascade over the sides of the planter.

Caring for Containers

We all know that plants growing in containers need regular care to keep them in good condition. But the containers need care, too.

You will need to clean pots, especially those made of clay, every two or three years, when fertilizer salts and, in regions where the water is hard, lime deposits start to build up around the rim of the pot. If enough of these deposits accumulate, they can harm plants. Soak the empty pots in water overnight to loosen salt deposits and caked-on soil. Then scrub them in soapy water and rinse thoroughly with clear water.

If you want to reuse a clay pot that has held a diseased plant, after you clean it soak it for several hours in a solution of one part liquid chlorine bleach to nine parts water.

September

Propagation

There are several ways to start new plants besides growing them from seeds. These techniques are collectively known as vegetative propagation. In vegetative propagation, a part of a mature plant is made to form roots and shoots and grow into a new plant that is an exact genetic duplicate of the parent plant. Some methods of vegetative propagation that are relatively easy for home gardeners to use are division, cuttings, and layering.

Division

Many perennials and bulbs spread by means of underground rhizomes and offsets. When the clump of plants or bulbs becomes too crowded, growth is less vigorous and fewer, smaller flowers are produced. Periodic division keeps these perennials and bulbs vigorous and free-flowering. Here's how to do it.

Perennials are divided when they are not in bloom. Summer and fall bloomers are usually divided in spring; spring-flowering perennials are divided in fall or, in cold climates, when they finish blooming. Do fall division four to six weeks before the first hard frost is likely, so the new plants can send roots out into the soil before they enter winter dormancy.

First cut back the stems to the ground. Remove the topsoil around the plant to expose the crowns. Drive a shovel into the soil in a circle around the plant, well away from the crowns. Then push the shovel at an angle under the roots, and lift the plant out of the ground. Try to leave intact as many roots as possible. Pull apart the clump of crowns, or cut it apart with a sharp knife to create several smaller crowns, each of which contains a number of eyes (growth buds). If the plant forms a large mass of crowns, get a friend and push two spading forks back to back into the center of the clump; lever the handles back and forth to pry the clump apart. If the clump of roots is thick and woody, as bearded iris will be when it has long been neglected, you may have to chop the mass into pieces with a hatchet.

Remove and discard the tough old roots from the center of the clump and replant the younger, stronger outer roots.

Replant the divisions right away so they do not dry out. Most plants should be replanted at the same depth they were growing before division.

To divide bulbs, dig the crowded clumps after the plants have bloomed and the foliage yellows. For true bulbs, like narcissus, simply separate the offsets from the parent bulb and replant them all.

For scaly bulbs such as lilies, remove the scales from around the outside of the parent bulb. Replant the parent, and set the scales, pointed end up, in containers of moist vermiculite. They will produce little bulblets which you can then plant in the garden to form new plants that will bloom in several years. Corms, such as gladiolus and crocus, are handled similarly, except that the old parent corm is discarded; detach the baby corms and replant them.

Clumps of tuberous roots like those of dahlias can be cut apart so that each division includes an eye and part of the old stem.

Cuttings

Cuttings can be taken from the stems, leaves, and roots of many perennials, annuals, shrubs, and trees. Stem cuttings are the most familiar and easiest to work with. Softwood, or green, cuttings are taken from young, green stems while the plant is actively growing. Sometimes these cuttings are called slips, when they are side shoots that can be separated (slipped) from the stem without the use of a knife. Hardwood cuttings are taken from stems when the season's growth has matured (hardened) and the plant is dormant. Use a sharp knife to take softwood cuttings, and pruning shears to take hardwood cuttings.

Softwood Cuttings

Take softwood cuttings when plants are about halfway through this year's growing season. Late spring is the time to take softwood cuttings from summer- and fall-blooming perennials. Take cuttings from spring-blooming perennials, trees, and shrubs in summer, and cuttings from annuals to grow indoors over winter in late summer or early fall.

Choose stems that are neither very young and soft nor old and woody; the stems should be firm but flexible, able to bend without crushing or snapping. Young side shoots of medium vigor, two to six inches long, are ideal. Cut the shoot at its base, without taking along a "heel" from the main stem (in most cases). If there are no side shoots small enough to use, take cuttings from the tips of longer shoots, cutting directly below a leaf or leaf node.

Place the cuttings in moist rooting medium (equal parts of peat and perlite or vermiculite) as soon as you cut them. To plant, pull out each cutting, remove the bottom leaves and insert the stem into the medium to about one-third of its length. Keep the medium evenly moist until the cuttings root, and give them lots of light.

Hardwood Cuttings

Take hardwood cuttings in fall when the leaves have dropped. Use the ends of branches or new canes grown during the current year. Cut the shoots into pieces six to ten inches long, if possible making the bottom cut just below a node and the top cut about one-fourth inch above a bud. Cut the bottom straight and the top on a slant so you will remember which end is which—it's important.

Tie the cuttings in bundles and store them over winter in a cold frame or foot-deep trench; stand the cuttings upright during storage and cover them completely with sand.

In spring, plant the cuttings outdoors as soon as the ground can be worked, in loose, porous, well-drained soil. Plant in full sun about eight to nine inches apart, burying the cuttings to the top bud or pair of buds. Water to settle the soil and do not let the soil dry out until the cuttings root, about three months later.

Take cuttings from conifers in either spring or fall, whichever works better for you—the experts disagree about the best time.

Layering

Layering allows you to root branches of woody plants while they are still attached to the parent plant. It is used for vines and shrubs with flexible stems. Layering works best in light, loose soil rich in organic matter. You can improve the soil around plants you want to layer by carefully removing several inches of topsoil, mixing it with compost, peat moss, and sand, then replacing it.

Use healthy, one-year-old shoots for layering. If you want to layer an old, neglected plant, prune it to encourage new growth, and wait until next year to layer it. Do the layering procedure in spring, as soon as the soil can be worked, while the plant is still dormant.

Insert the tip of a spade into the ground six inches deep beneath the branch to be layered, and wiggle it back and forth to make a narrow slit. Bend the branch down to the ground and push it into the slit; hold it in place with U-shaped pins, forked twigs, or stones. Bend the tip of the stem upward so three to six inches of it are above ground. Cover the buried part of the stem with a mixture of soil and compost, and pack it well. Water.

How long it takes for the buried stem to form roots depends upon the plant—rooting can take three months to three years. Pull gently on the stem to see if roots have formed; if you feel resistance the stem has probably rooted. Sever the stem from the parent and transplant the baby, keeping it watered and protected from hot sun until it establishes itself in its new home.

Water new and established plants deeply if weather is dry, to prepare for winter. Begin fall cleanup. Set up mouse guards or wrap trunks of young trees. Set up windbreaks for plants in windy locations. Stake young trees to hold them in place during winter storms.

See Zone 3

Plant trees, shrubs, and evergreens. Water new and established plants deeply during dry weather. Begin fall cleanup. Set up mouse guards or wrap trunks of young trees. Set up windbreaks for plants in windy locations. Stake young trees to hold them in place during winter storms. Watch for pests and signs of disease.

Prepare planting holes for trees, shrubs, and evergreens. Water plants deeply during dry weather to prepare for winter. Lay fresh mulch around acid-lovers. Begin fall cleanup. Set up mouse guards or wrap trunks of young trees. Set up windbreaks for plants in windy locations. Watch for pests and signs of disease.

Prepare planting holes for evergreen trees and shrubs, and spring-blooming shrubs and vines. Water plants deeply in dry weather. Trim hedges. Lay fresh mulch around acid-lovers. Watch for pests and signs of disease.

Prepare planting holes for trees, shrubs, and vines. Water plants deeply in dry weather. Fertilize tender trees and shrubs. Trim hedges. Prune weak and damaged growth from trees and large shrubs. Take cuttings from evergreens. Watch for pests and signs of disease.

Keep roots of mail-order plants moist until planting time. Prepare planting holes for trees, shrubs, and vines. Water plants deeply in dry weather, especially new plantings and spring bloomers setting buds. Fertilize tender trees and shrubs. Trim hedges. Prune weak and damaged growth. Take cuttings from evergreens. Watch for pests and signs of disease.

See Zone 9

Roses	Lawns & Ground Covers	Zone
Water if weather is dry. Clip off new growth that has not yet hardened. Mound soil around base of plants for winter protection.	Aerate lawn if not done in spring. Fertilize established lawns or top-dress with compost if not yet done. Plant ground covers early in month. Water new plantings regularly until ground freezes.	*1-3*
Water if weather is dry. Clip off new growth that has not yet hardened. Mound soil around base of shrub roses for winter protection. Watch for pests and signs of disease.	Plant ground covers early in month. Aerate lawn if not done in spring. Fertilize established lawns or top-dress with compost if not yet done. Water new plantings regularly until ground freezes.	*4*
Water as needed until ground freezes. Clip off new growth that has not yet hardened. Mound soil around base of roses for winter protection. Pick up dropped leaves in rose garden. Watch for pests and signs of disease.	Plant ground covers. Aerate lawn if not done in spring. Fertilize established lawns or top-dress with compost if not yet done. Keep new plantings moist until ground freezes. Mow grass if still necessary.	*5*
Prepare planting holes for new roses. Water if weather is dry. Watch for pests and signs of disease. Plant roses when weather cools.	Plant ground covers and ornamental grasses. Aerate lawn if not done in spring. Fertilize established lawns or top-dress with compost. Water new plantings regularly. Mow grass weekly or as needed. Divide crowded clumps of ornamental grasses.	*6*
Prepare planting holes for new roses. Fertilize established plants for last time six weeks before first expected fall frost. Water if weather is dry. Watch for pests and signs of disease. Pick up fallen leaves.	See Zone 6	*7*
Prepare planting holes for new roses. Continue to weed, water, deadhead, and fertilize established plants. Watch for pests and signs of disease. Pick up fallen leaves.	Plant ground covers and ornamental grasses. In northern part of zone, reseed bare or thin spots in lawn; seed new lawns. Fertilize established lawns or top-dress with compost. Aerate lawn if not done in spring; de-thatch if necessary. Water new plantings regularly, established lawns as needed. Mow grass weekly or as needed.	*8*
See Zone 8	Seed or lay sod for cool-season lawn grasses. Keep new lawns moist; water established lawns as needed. Aerate lawn if not done in spring; de-thatch if necessary. Fertilize established lawns or top-dress with compost. Mow grass weekly or as needed.	*9*
See Zone 8	See Zone 9	*10-11*

Perennials

Bulbs

1-3 Cut back perennials to three to four inches. Water during dry weather until ground freezes. Edge beds and borders. Clean up all plant debris from garden. Prepare planting areas for next spring.

Plant crocus, narcissus, and other spring bulbs, and lily-of-the-valley. Dig dahlias after first frost.

4 Fertilize mums just before buds open. Cut back earlier bloomers to three to four inches. Water during dry weather until ground freezes. Edge beds and borders. Clean up all plant debris from garden. Prepare planting areas for next spring.

Plant crocus and other early spring bulbs; plant lily-of-the-valley. Dig gladiolus when they finish blooming; dig dahlias after first frost.

5 Plant perennials for next year. Fertilize mums just before buds open. Cut back earlier bloomers when topgrowth begins to die back. Water new plantings regularly. Edge beds and borders. Clean up plant debris from garden. Dig and divide crowded spring and summer bloomers. Prepare planting areas for next spring.

Late in month, plant crocus and other early spring bulbs; plant lily-of-the-valley. Dig gladiolus when they finish blooming; dig dahlias after first frost.

6 See Zone 5

Late in month, plant crocus and other early spring bulbs; plant lily-of-the-valley. Dig gladiolus when they finish blooming. Cut lilies back to ground when stalks die back.

7 Plant perennials for next year. Fertilize mums for last time just before buds open. Cut back earlier bloomers when topgrowth begins to die back. Water new plantings regularly. Edge beds and borders. Clean up plant debris from garden. Dig and divide crowded spring and summer bloomers. Watch for pests and signs of disease.

Plant autumn-blooming bulbs; plant lilies. Order hardy bulbs for fall planting if not already done. Check stakes on gladiolus and dahlias. Cut lilies back to ground when stalks die back. Watch for pests and signs of disease.

8 Plant perennials for next year. Fertilize late bloomers; feed mums for last time just before buds open. Cut back earlier bloomers when topgrowth begins to die back. Weed as needed. Water new plantings regularly; established plants as needed. Take cuttings to start new plants. Edge beds and borders. Dig and divide crowded clumps of earlier bloomers. Watch for pests and signs of disease.

Plant autumn-blooming bulbs; plant lilies. Order hardy bulbs for fall planting; store them in refrigerator until planting time. Prepare soil for later planting. Deadhead faded flowers. Check stakes on tall dahlias and gladiolus. Cut lilies back to ground when stalks die back. Watch for pests and signs of disease.

9 Thin and transplant perennials sown last month. Fertilize tropical plants and late bloomers. Cut back earlier bloomers when topgrowth begins to die back. Weed as needed. Water new plantings regularly, established plants as needed. Take cuttings to start new plants. Edge beds and borders. Watch for pests and signs of disease.

Plant autumn-blooming bulbs; plant tender spring bloomers; plant lilies. Order hardy bulbs for fall planting; store them in refrigerator until planting time. Prepare soil for later planting. Deadhead faded flowers. Check stakes on tall glads and dahlias. Cut lilies back to ground when stalks die back. Watch for pests and signs of disease.

10-11 Thin and transplant perennials sown last month. Fertilize tropical plants and late bloomers. Cut back earlier bloomers when topgrowth begins to die back. Weed and water as needed. Take cuttings to start new plants. Edge beds and borders. Watch for pests and signs of disease.

See Zone 9

Pull up annuals when killed by frost. Clean up beds and borders. Continue to weed, water, and deadhead while plants are still blooming.

Take cuttings of coleus and other annuals to pot up for winter houseplants. Pull up annuals when killed by frost. Clean up beds and borders. Continue to weed, water, and deadhead while plants are still blooming.

Continue to deadhead, weed, water, and fertilize plants still in bloom. Take cuttings of coleus, geraniums, and other annuals to pot up for winter houseplants. Pull up annuals when killed by frost. Clean up empty beds and borders.

Continue to deadhead, weed, water, and fertilize plants still in bloom. Take cuttings of coleus, geraniums, and other annuals to pot up for winter houseplants. Pull up annuals when plants fatigue or are killed by frost. Clean up empty beds and borders.

Direct-sow hardy annuals for flowers next spring; sow pansies in garden or cold frame. Continue to deadhead, weed, water, and fertilize plants still in bloom. Take cuttings of coleus, geraniums, and other annuals to pot up for winter houseplants. Pull up annuals when plants fatigue. Clean up empty beds and borders.

See Zone 7

Direct-sow hardy annuals for winter flowers; sow sweet peas; sow pansies in garden or cold frame. Continue to deadhead, weed, water, and fertilize plants still in bloom. Take cuttings of coleus, geraniums, and other annuals to pot up for winter houseplants. Pull up annuals when plants fatigue. Clean up empty beds and borders in preparation for replanting.

See Zone 9

	Container Gardens	Vegetables & Herbs
1-3	Clean out containers and compost plants killed by frost. Continue to care for plants still growing. If any plants are diseased, dispose of plants (do not compost) and disinfect pots.	Cover tender crops on cold nights to extend harvest through first few frosts. Keep up with harvest. When frost kills plants, remove them to the compost pile. Prepare storage areas for root crops. Continue to care for plants still growing. Turn compost pile. Watch for pests and signs of disease.
4	See Zone 3	Keep up with harvest. Cover tender crops on cold nights to extend harvest through first few frosts. Prepare storage areas for root crops. When frost kills plants, remove them to compost pile. Continue to care for plants still growing. Turn compost pile. Watch for signs of pests and disease.
5	Continue to care for plants still growing, but do not fertilize woody plants until next spring. When frost kills plants, clean out containers and put contents on compost pile. If any plants are diseased, dispose of plants (do not compost) and disinfect pots.	Keep up with harvest. Thin seedlings planted last month in cold frame. Prepare storage areas for root crops. Continue to weed, water, and fertilize. Turn compost pile. Watch for pests and signs of disease.
6	See Zone 5	Keep up with harvest. Plant cool-weather crops in cold frame. Thin seedlings planted last month in cold frame and garden. Prepare storage areas for root crops. Continue to weed, water, and fertilize. Remove spent plants. Clean up empty areas of garden. Turn compost pile. Watch for pests and signs of disease.
7	Harvest vegetables and herbs, cut flowers from containers. Continue to deadhead, water, and fertilize container plants, but stop fertilizing woody plants until next spring.	Keep up with harvest. Plant cool-weather plants in garden or cold frame. Thin seedlings planted last month. Continue to weed, water, and fertilize as needed. Remove spent plants. Clean up empty areas in garden. Turn compost pile. Watch for pests and signs of disease.
8	Harvest vegetables and herbs, cut flowers from containers. Continue to deadhead, water, and fertilize container plants.	See Zone 7
9	Sow hardy annuals and cool-weather vegetables in containers. Harvest vegetables and herbs, cut flowers from containers. Continue to deadhead, water, and fertilize container plants.	Keep up with harvest. Plant cool-weather plants in garden or sow indoors. Transplant out seedlings started earlier. Continue to weed, water, and fertilize as needed. Check supports for climbing plants. Remove spent plants. Clean up dropped leaves and other debris. Turn compost pile. Watch for pests and signs of disease.
10-11	See Zone 9	See Zone 9

Fruit

Harvest ripe fruit. Cut back old bramble canes. Mow tall grass and weeds in orchards. Clean up dropped fruit and leaves. Place mouse guards around trunks of young trees. When soil freezes, mulch trees in a ring eight to twelve inches from trunk.

See Zone 3

Harvest ripe fruit. Mow tall grass and weeds in orchards. Clean up dropped fruit and leaves. Prune wood damaged by disease; disinfect tools. Watch for pests and signs of disease.

See Zone 5

Harvest ripe fruit. Plant strawberry runners rooted in pots. Water during dry weather. Clean up dropped fruit and leaves. Watch for pests and signs of disease.

Harvest ripe fruit. Wrap trunks of young trees to prevent sunscald (see page 79). Clean up dropped fruit and leaves. Watch for pests and signs of disease.

Fertilize fruit trees and bushes after harvest ends. Fertilize citrus. Water as needed. Layer berries to start new plants. Clean up dropped fruit and leaves. Watch for pests and signs of disease.

See Zone 9

Plants to Grow from Cuttings

Softwood Cuttings

Annuals
Wax begonia, geranium, coleus, impatiens.

Perennials
Ajuga, baby's breath, blanketflower, butterfly weed, campanula, candytuft, chrysanthemum, delphinium, dianthus, English ivy, false rockcress, forget-me-not, lavender, mints, oregano, periwinkle, phlox, rock cress, rosemary, sedum, tarragon, thyme, veronica.

Shrubs and Trees
Abelia, barberry, beauty bush, broom, boxwood, butterfly bush, camellia, flowering cherry, citrus, clematis, cotoneaster, daphne, deutzia, dogwood, euonymus, forsythia, fothergilla, gardenia, hibiscus, holly, honeysuckle, hydrangea, hardy kiwi, lilac, magnolia, maple, mock orange, Russian olive, autumn olive, picris, flowering quince, eastern redbud, deciduous rhododendrons, species roses, sourwood, spiraea, sweet gum, sweet pepperbush, viburnum, weigela, willow, winter hazel, wisteria, witch hazel.

Hardwood Cuttings
Alder, arborvitae, evergreen azalea, beauty bush, camellia, crape myrtle, currant, deutzia, euonymus, fig, fire thorn, forsythia, gooseberry, grape, holly, honeysuckle, hydrangea, hardy kiwi, mock orange, Russian olive, raspberry, evergreen rhododendron, climbing and rambler roses, rose of Sharon, sweet shrub, willow, yew.

Plants to Layer

Blackberry, cotoneaster, forsythia, gooseberry, grape, hemlock, periwinkle, raspberry, spiraea, strawberry, witch hazel.

October

Extending the Growing Season

Autumn brings mild weather and a welcome relief from the heat in the southern part of the country. But in the north, the growing season is winding down. Gardeners in the far North have already had their first frost by October; it can come as early as mid-September in northern New England and the upper Midwest. If you want to get more from your garden than your natural growing season allows, try some of the methods described below to extend the season.

There are a number of ways to stretch the growing season past the first frosts in fall; the same techniques can also let you get an early start in spring. One strategy is to protect plants on cold nights when frost is likely. You can cover plants individually or in groups.

There are several types of covers you can use on rows or entire garden beds. Probably the easiest to use are "floating" row covers made of spun-bonded polyester. This lightweight material rests right on top of the plants without weighting them down. It keeps light frost (and insects) off the plants while letting in light, air, and water. Garden blankets made of this material are available in several sizes.

Clear plastic row covers allow you to create a protected environment right in the garden in spring and fall. If you decide to make your own plastic tunnels, be sure to use polyethylene, which allows plants to respire. Other kinds of plastics could suffocate them. Stretch the plastic over wire hoops or some other sort of framework to make a tunnel that does not come in contact with plant leaves. On sunny days the tunnel will need ventilation; you can either roll up the sides or cut slits in the plastic along the sides.

A classic English device for protecting a few plants is called a cloche. A cloche is a sort of mini-greenhouse made of two pieces of glass fastened together at the top with a special metal clip, to form an A-frame structure. You supply your own glass and purchase the clips, named Rumsey clips after their inventor. Other wire fittings allow you to add vertical sides to the A-frame for extra height; the cloche then becomes a barn-shaped structure.

If you have tall or climbing plants to protect, you can make a tent from a sheet of polyethylene draped over a wire strung between two poles.

For last-minute emergencies, like that unseasonably early cold snap, you can pop covers over individual plants. These covers are easy to use, but you must set them out in the evening and remove them the next morn-

ing. They don't hold much heat at night, and they would overheat if left in place on a sunny day, but in a pinch they can save those last few tomatoes or a few favorite flowers.

The French market gardeners of times past covered their plants with glass bell jars. A less breakable alternative is hot caps made of plastic, cardboard, or heavy waxed paper. Or cut the bottoms from gallon-sized plastic milk jugs and set the jugs over the plants. Leave the caps off to allow ventilation.

Cardboard boxes, upside down peach baskets, and half-gallon cardboard milk cartons can also be pressed into service as plant covers. They're effective, if not aesthetically pleasing.

If you live in farm country and have access to old-fashioned bales of hay, you can throw together a sort of temporary cold frame to protect a group of cherished plants. Stack bales of hay around the plants, and cover the top with an old storm window or a sheet of plastic with the edges weighted down with soil or rocks.

More versatile than any of these simple protection devices is a true cold frame. A cold frame will let you extend the growing season for lots of different purposes.

Cold Frames

A cold frame can extend your growing season by weeks or even months. The cold frame is basically a bottomless box set atop soil where plants are grown. The frame has a glass or plastic cover that lets in sunlight; inside the frame the light is converted to heat, which warms the air and soil inside the structure. You can build a simple cold frame for yourself from scrap lumber and one or more old storm windows, or you can purchase one.

Use the cold frame to start spring plants several weeks before they could be started in the garden, and to harden-off transplants. In autumn, the cold frame allows you to grow cool-weather vegetables for a later harvest than would be possible in the unprotected outdoor garden. You can also use the frame to root cuttings, or to start biennials and hardy perennials from seed, to plant out in the garden in their second year. In summer, remove the lid and turn the cold frame into a nursery for starting plants that will be later transplanted into the main garden. The size and height of the cold frame will determine what you can grow.

The best location for a cold frame is one that receives full sun all day, and faces south. A south-facing spot that is protected on the north side—along the south-facing wall of a garage, perhaps—would be ideal.

You can use garden soil in the cold frame, as long as it is of good quality. But the best results are achieved with soil that is porous and well-drained, as well as fertile. An excellent soil for a cold frame is a mixture of equal parts of good garden soil, compost or leaf mold, composted manure, and perlite or vermiculite.

On sunny days when the outdoor temperature rises above about 45 degrees F, you must ventilate the cold frame or it will get too hot inside for plants. Open the lid partway to let in cool, fresh air, and to let out excess moisture that builds up and can lead to damping-off or fungus diseases. You will have to learn by trial and error how much to open the lid and for how long—too much cold air will shock and damage the plants. If you're away at work all day, you may want to invest in an automatic opening device for the cold frame lid.

Prepare trees and shrubs for winter. Stake young trees to prevent wind damage. Install mouse guards around trunks of young trees. When soil freezes, mulch new plantings to prevent frost heaving.

1-3

Take hardwood cuttings after leaves drop. Prepare trees and shrubs for winter. Stake young trees to prevent wind damage. Install mouse guards around trunks of young trees. When soil freezes, mulch new plantings to prevent frost heaving. Rake up healthy leaves to make compost.

4

Plant evergreens; plant deciduous trees and shrubs when leaves have fallen. Water new plantings and established evergreens weekly in dry weather. Take hardwood cuttings after leaves drop. Prune climbers and fasten securely to their supports. Stake young trees to prevent winter wind damage. Install mouse guards around trunks of young trees. Rake up healthy leaves to make compost.

5

See Zone 5

6

See Zone 5

7

Plant evergreens; plant deciduous trees, shrubs, and vines when leaves have fallen. Water new plantings and established evergreens weekly in dry weather. Stake new trees. Take hardwood cuttings after leaves drop. Prune climbers and fasten securely to their supports. Wrap trunks of young trees to prevent sunscald. Rake up healthy leaves to make compost.

8

Plant evergreens and vines. Fertilize evergreens, trees, and shrubs that bloom in spring. Water new plants regularly and established plantings deeply in dry weather. Stake new trees. Watch for pests and signs of disease.

9

See Zone 9

10-11

	Roses	Lawns & Ground Covers
1-3	Prune shrub roses when they go dormant. When ground freezes, mulch deeply.	Water newly planted ground covers if necessary until ground freezes.
4	Prune shrub roses when they go dormant. When ground freezes, mulch deeply. Remove ramblers and climbers from supports, lay canes gently on the ground, and cover with soil mound, evergreen boughs, or thick mulch.	See Zone 3
5	Water as needed until ground freezes. Mound soil around base of plants for winter protection. Detach ramblers and climbers from supports, gently lay canes on the ground, and cover with soil mound, evergreen boughs, or thick mulch. Clean up rose garden; dispose of any diseased leaves.	Water newly planted ground covers if necessary until ground freezes. Edge lawn and dig out dandelions and other weeds.
6	Plant roses. Water regularly until ground freezes. Mound soil around base of plants for winter protection. Prune ramblers and climbers and fasten firmly to their supports, or detach canes gently, lay on ground, and cover with evergreen boughs, or thick mulch. Clean up rose garden; dispose of any diseased leaves.	Water newly planted ground covers and ornamental grasses regularly if weather is dry. Edge lawn, dig out dandelions and other weeds. Mow lawn if still necessary.
7	Plant roses. Water regularly until ground freezes. Prune ramblers and climbers and fasten firmly to their supports. Clean up rose garden; dispose of any diseased leaves. Watch for pests and signs of disease.	Plant ground covers and ornamental grasses. Water new plantings regularly in dry weather. Fertilize established lawns or top-dress with compost if not done last month. Mow lawn when necessary. Divide crowded clumps of ornamental grasses.
8	Plant roses. Water regularly as plants become established. Prune climbers and ramblers and fasten firmly to their supports. Clean up dropped leaves around roses; dispose of any diseased leaves. Watch for pests and signs of disease.	Plant ground covers and ornamental grasses. Overseed summer lawns with ryegrass; sow cool-weather lawns, reseed thin or bare spots. Water new plantings regularly if weather is dry. Fertilize established lawns or top-dress with compost if not done last month. Mow lawn when necessary. Divide crowded clumps of ornamental grasses.
9	Water roses if necessary during dry weather. Prune dead or damaged growth. Clean up dropped leaves around roses; dispose of any diseased leaves. Watch for pests and signs of disease.	See Zone 8
10-11	See Zone 9	See Zone 8

Perennials

Notes

Cut back perennials to three to four inches if not done last month. Water during dry weather until ground freezes; ease off as plants go dormant. Clean up all plant debris from beds and borders. Mulch perennials thickly when ground is frozen.

Cut back perennials to three to four inches if not already done; cut back mums when they finish blooming. Move perennials not reliably hardy into cold frame. Water during dry weather until ground freezes; ease off as plants go dormant. Clean up all plant debris from beds and borders. Mulch perennials thickly when ground is frozen.

Cut back perennials to three to four inches; cut back mums when they finish blooming. Move perennials not reliably hardy into cold frame. Water during dry weather; ease off as plants begin to go dormant. Weed and clean up plant debris from beds and borders.

See Zone 5

Plant new perennials; divide and replant crowded clumps of spring bloomers. Water new plants regularly, established plants as needed. Cut back perennials when topgrowth starts to die back; cut back mums when they finish blooming. Move perennials not reliably hardy into cold frame. Weed and clean up plant debris from beds and borders.

Plant new perennials; divide and transplant crowded clumps of spring bloomers. Water new plants regularly, established plants as needed. Cut back perennials to two to three inches when they finish blooming, earlier bloomers when topgrowth starts to die back. Weed and clean up plant debris from beds and borders.

See Zone 8

See Zone 8

Bulbs

Annuals

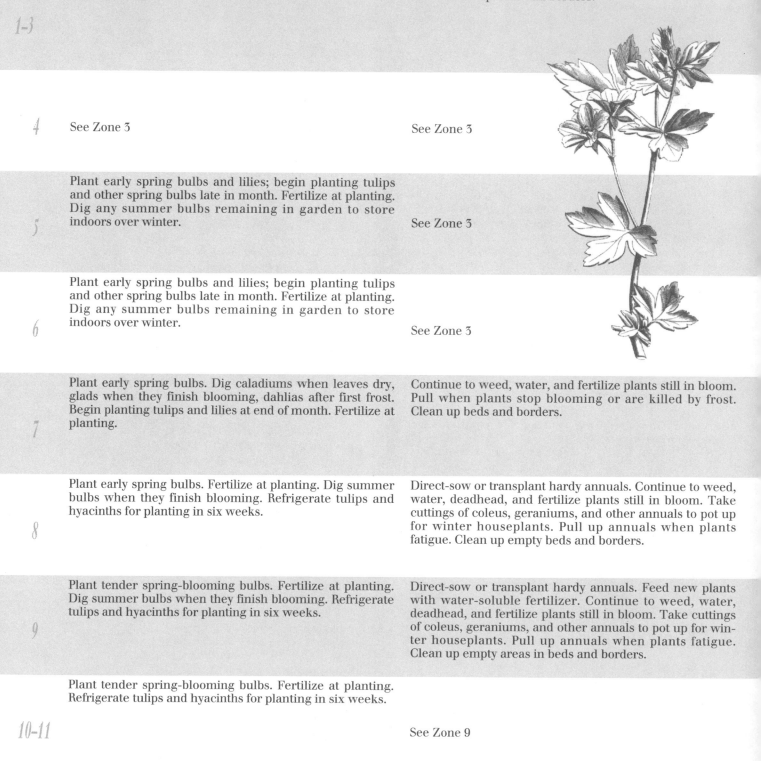

1-3

Plant spring bulbs and lilies before ground freezes. Fertilize at planting.

Pull annuals when plants stop blooming or are killed by frost. Clean up beds and borders.

4

See Zone 3

See Zone 3

5

Plant early spring bulbs and lilies; begin planting tulips and other spring bulbs late in month. Fertilize at planting. Dig any summer bulbs remaining in garden to store indoors over winter.

See Zone 3

6

Plant early spring bulbs and lilies; begin planting tulips and other spring bulbs late in month. Fertilize at planting. Dig any summer bulbs remaining in garden to store indoors over winter.

See Zone 3

7

Plant early spring bulbs. Dig caladiums when leaves dry, glads when they finish blooming, dahlias after first frost. Begin planting tulips and lilies at end of month. Fertilize at planting.

Continue to weed, water, and fertilize plants still in bloom. Pull when plants stop blooming or are killed by frost. Clean up beds and borders.

8

Plant early spring bulbs. Fertilize at planting. Dig summer bulbs when they finish blooming. Refrigerate tulips and hyacinths for planting in six weeks.

Direct-sow or transplant hardy annuals. Continue to weed, water, deadhead, and fertilize plants still in bloom. Take cuttings of coleus, geraniums, and other annuals to pot up for winter houseplants. Pull up annuals when plants fatigue. Clean up empty beds and borders.

9

Plant tender spring-blooming bulbs. Fertilize at planting. Dig summer bulbs when they finish blooming. Refrigerate tulips and hyacinths for planting in six weeks.

Direct-sow or transplant hardy annuals. Feed new plants with water-soluble fertilizer. Continue to weed, water, deadhead, and fertilize plants still in bloom. Take cuttings of coleus, geraniums, and other annuals to pot up for winter houseplants. Pull up annuals when plants fatigue. Clean up empty areas in beds and borders.

10-11

Plant tender spring-blooming bulbs. Fertilize at planting. Refrigerate tulips and hyacinths for planting in six weeks.

See Zone 9

Container Gardens	Vegetables & Herbs	Zone
Empty clay pots and bring indoors for winter to avoid cracking. Clean out containers and put contents on compost pile when frost kills plants.	Spread compost or other organic matter over garden. Update crop performance records. Mulch perennial herbs when ground freezes. Take down stakes and trellises: clean and store for next year.	1-3
See Zone 3	When fall harvest ends, plant cover crop or spread compost or other organic material over garden. Update crop performance records. Mulch perennial herbs when ground freezes. Take down stakes and trellises; clean and store for next year.	4
Empty clay pots and bring indoors for winter to avoid cracking. Clean out containers and put contents on compost pile when frost kills plants. Continue to care for mums and other plants still growing in containers.	Harvest fall crops as they become ready; harvest winter squash before first heavy frost. Plant cover crop or spread compost or other organic material in empty parts of garden. Update crop performance records. Take down stakes and trellises; clean and store for next year.	5
Continue to care for mums and other plants still growing in containers. Harvest late salad greens and herbs from containers. Clean out containers and put contents on compost pile when frost kills plants. Empty clay pots and bring indoors for winter to avoid cracking.	Harvest fall crops as they become ready; harvest winter squash before first heavy frost. Protect plants when frost is expected. Thickly mulch root crops to be left in garden. Take down stakes and trellises; clean and store for next year. Plant cover crop or spread compost or other organic material in empty parts of garden.	6
See Zone 6	Harvest last of summer crops; harvest fall crops. Transplant young salad greens and herbs to cold frame for later harvest. Protect plants in garden when frost is expected. Pull spent plants and compost. Turn compost pile. Thickly mulch root crops to be left in garden. Remove stakes and trellises; clean and store for next year. Plant cover crop or spread compost in empty parts of garden.	7
Harvest salad greens and herbs, cut flowers from containers. Continue to care for mums and other plants still growing in containers. Stop fertilizing woody plants. Watch for pests and signs of disease.	Keep up with harvest. Plant cool-weather crops in garden or cold frame. Continue to weed, water, and fertilize as needed. Pull spent plants and put on compost pile. Turn compost pile. Mulch root crops to be left in garden. Plant cover crop or spread compost in empty parts of garden. Watch for pests and signs of disease.	8
Harvest vegetables and herbs, cut flowers from containers. Plant hardy annuals and cool-weather vegetables. Continue to care for mums and other plants still growing in containers. Watch for pests and signs of disease.	Keep up with harvest. Plant cool-weather crops in garden or cold frame. Continue to weed, water, and fertilize as needed. Pull spent plants and put on compost pile. Turn compost pile. Take cuttings of perennial herbs to start new plants. Watch for pests and signs of disease.	9
See Zone 9	See Zone 9	10-11

Fruit

1-3

Clean up dropped fruit and leaves. Place mouse guards around trunks of young trees. Wrap young tree trunks to prevent sunscald. Take down grapevines, lay gently on ground, and mulch after heavy frost but before ground freezes. When soil freezes, mulch trees in a ring eight to twelve inches from trunk.

4

Fertilize berries and brambles or top-dress with compost. Clean up dropped fruit and leaves. Place mouse guards around trunks of young trees. Wrap young tree trunks to prevent sunscald. Take down grapevines, lay gently on ground, and mulch after heavy frost but before ground freezes. When soil freezes, mulch trees in a ring eight to twelve inches from trunk.

5

Water young trees deeply before ground freezes. Fertilize berries and brambles or top-dress with compost. Clean up dropped fruit and leaves; compost if healthy. Place mouse guards around trunks of young trees. Wrap young tree trunks to prevent sunscald. Cover strawberries if temperature goes below 20 degrees F. After hard frost, thin and cut back brambles.

6

Harvest ripe fruit. Water young trees deeply. Clean up dropped fruit and leaves; compost if healthy. Place mouse guards around trunks of young trees. After hard frost, thin and cut back brambles.

7

Harvest ripe fruit. Plant berry bushes; finish planting strawberry runners. Water young trees and new plants deeply. Clean up dropped fruit and leaves; compost if healthy. Place mouse guards around trunks of young trees.

8

Harvest ripe fruit. Plant berry bushes; finish planting strawberry runners. Water young trees and new plants deeply. Clean up dropped fruit and leaves; compost if healthy. Thin and cut back brambles when they finish bearing. Watch for pests and signs of disease.

9

Harvest ripe fruit. Plant berry bushes and fruit trees. Water new plants deeply. Clean up dropped fruit and leaves; compost if healthy. Thin and cut back brambles when they finish bearing. Watch for pests and signs of disease.

10-11

See Zone 9

How to Store Leftover Seeds

If you have unused seeds left over from this year's garden, you don't have to throw them out. Many seeds will remain viable for two or three years, or even longer, if kept in the right kind of conditions. To save unused seeds, close the packet and reseal it or roll it up and fasten with a rubber band. Place the packets in a glass jar with a tight-fitting lid. As an extra precaution you can pour a few tablespoons of powdered milk or silica gel crystals (used to dry flowers) in the jar to absorb moisture. Screw on the cap tightly, and put the jar in a cool, dry place. The basement or refrigerator is a good place to store many kinds of seeds.

Next spring, test the seeds for viability as described on page 14 before you plant them.

Lifting and Storing Tender Bulbs

When the first fall frosts arrive, it's time for tender summer-blooming bulbs to come out of the ground in all but frost-free gardens. Tuberoses and tuberous begonias cannot tolerate any frost at all, and must be brought indoors before even the first light frost strikes. But dahlias, Peruvian daffodils, gladiolus, and the rest can stay outdoors until the foliage begins to turn brown, or until the first light frost or two has occurred. Just be sure to get all your tender bulbs indoors before the first heavy frost, when crowns and the bulbs themselves could be damaged.

To dig the bulbs, loosen the soil around the plant, then carefully lift the entire plant with a spading fork or shovel. Leave in place the soil clinging to the bulbs. Let the bulbs dry in a cool, dark, airy place where they will not be exposed to frost. Remove dried leaves and stems when they fall off. A few days later, brush the dry soil from the bulbs. Pack them in newspaper or tissue paper, or dry peat moss or vermiculite, and store in a dark, dry place where the temperature will not fall below 50 degrees F.

Make sure the bulbs are dry on the surface before you put them into storage, or they will be likely to develop mold or rot. Check them periodically through the winter, and throw out any that feel soft or look moldy or mildewed. If the bulbs begin to wrinkle and dry out, mist them lightly with water.

November

Pruning

It's not enough to put plants in the ground in the garden or backyard landscape and expect them to grow unattended. Garden plants need care to help them achieve their ultimate potential. Other monthly introductions in this book have looked at a variety of cultural practices—watering, fertilizing, pest control, and other techniques. This month offers an overview of basic pruning.

You may think of pruning only in terms of trees, but many plants grow better when pruned. Evergreen hedges and foundation plants, woody vines, conifers, and flowering shrubs all need pruning from time to time. Herbaceous perennials do, too: deadheading faded flowers is a form of pruning. Plants being trained to unnatural shapes, such as espaliered trees and topiaries, need frequent pruning and training to maintain their shape.

Prune woody plants to remove damaged and weak growth, to get rid of water sprouts and suckers, to improve overall shape, or to enhance flowering or fruiting. You may also need to remove branches growing into utility wires, against a building, or elsewhere you don't want them, or to thin out growth to let more light get to plants growing below the trees. Pruning can eliminate crowded or crossed branches, or you can prune to shorten branches or shoots, or to encourage growth in a particu-

lar direction. For denser, more compact growth, prune to an inward-facing bud. For an open shape, prune to an outward-facing bud.

Most large trees and shrubs are pruned in late winter or early spring, when they are dormant and deciduous species are without leaves. Prune before buds swell and new growth begins. Some trees, such as dogwoods, birches, and maples, bleed a lot of sap when pruned in early spring, but the bleeding really does not harm the tree, and this is still generally the best time of year to prune them. Early spring is also a good time to prune evergreens, although most can be pruned just about anytime but late summer. (Pines are the exception; prune them when candles—new shoots—are no more than six inches long.) Shrubs that bloom in spring are best pruned when they finish blooming. Pruning them in early spring would remove flower buds and lessen the show.

In summer, prune to remove water sprouts and suckers, and to control the growth of unruly plants. You will also need to trim hedges, topiaries, and foundation plantings throughout the summer.

Try to avoid pruning trees and shrubs in fall, except to remove damaged or diseased wood. The new growth that will be stimulated by the pruning will not have time to harden fully before cold weather sets in, and will be susceptible to winter damage.

Learning proper pruning techniques is important, and I suggest you study a good book on the subject before starting.

For the sake of the tree's or shrub's health, don't remove more than a quarter of the total topgrowth at a time by pruning. Always work with sharp, clean tools.

When removing a branch, cut right along the outer edge of the "collar," the swollen area where the branch meets the trunk. Do not leave a stub of branch beyond the branch collar, and do not cut into the collar itself; both increase the possibility of insect damage or disease.

If you are taking off a big branch, it is best to make three separate cuts. Make the first cut one-third to halfway through the branch from the underside, six to twelve inches out from the collar. Make the second cut a few inches out from the first one, and cut all the way through the branch, starting from the top. The final cut is to remove the stub of the branch, flush with the collar; cut downward from the top of the branch. Experts today recommend that you do *not* seal the cuts with tree paint or wound sealer.

Pruning Fruit

Prune fruit trees in spring; apples and pears while dormant; and cherries, peaches, apricots, and plums later in spring, around the time they bloom. Fruit trees are pruned to a central-leader, modified-leader, or open-vase shape.

The central-leader form has a dominant vertical branch, and is often used for apples and pears. When you plant a young tree, choose one branch to be the leader, and three or four strong lateral branches evenly spaced around the trunk to form the basic structure, or scaffold, of the tree. Choose branches that grow at a wide angle from the trunk; sharply angled branches are more likely to crack under the weight of maturing fruit.

A modified leader is sometimes used for stone fruits. It begins the same as the central-leader form, but after several good scaffold limbs are chosen and developed, the top of the central leader is cut off.

The vase form is also used for peaches, plums, apricots, and cherries. An open-vase shape has well-spaced scaffold branches and no dominant central leader. When the tree is young, choose, for the scaffold, branches that grow out from the trunk at a wide angle.

As a rule, horizontal branches bear more fruit than more upright branches, and the upper side of the branch

produces more than the underside, which is shaded. Remember these characteristics when pruning.

Grapes and bramble fruits (raspberries and black-berries) are usually trained to grow on trellis wires. The way grapes are pruned depends upon the training system used. Grapevines are cut back each year, so that vigorous young canes can produce good crops of fruit. Bramble pruning depends upon the type of plant involved: some brambles bear fruit in early summer on two-year-old canes and in late summer on the current year's canes; others bear all their fruit on second-year growth. The easiest pruning method is to simply cut back half of all the canes during dormancy. More time-consuming, but more fruit-productive, is to cut the two-year-old canes back to the ground when they finish bearing. Or you can prune away all canes except for four or five per plant (or per foot of row) in early summer when they are six to ten inches tall.

Prune bush fruits—blueberries, currants, and gooseberries—in early spring while the plants are still dormant. Basically, pruning efforts should focus on removing old wood, crowded stems, and winter-damaged growth. The goal is to have vigorous young canes that have plenty of room to grow. Cut back to the ground blueberry stems larger than one inch in diameter, and stems of currants and gooseberries that are more than four years old.

Check winter protection for shrubs to make sure it's secure. If protecting plants with soil mounds at base, mulch when mounds have frozen. Spray evergreens with antidesiccant if not yet done, when temperature goes above 40 degrees F. Wrap trunks of young trees to prevent sunscald. Look for overwintering pests; remove and destroy.

Water evergreens deeply before ground freezes solid. Place winter protection, mouse guards, and windbreaks if not yet done. If protecting plants with soil mounds at base, mulch when mounds have frozen. Wrap trunks of young trees to prevent sunscald. Spray evergreens with antidesiccant if not yet done, when temperature is above 40 degrees F. Remove and destroy overwintering pests.

Water evergreens deeply before ground freezes. Fertilize deciduous and evergreen trees and shrubs when dormant. Wrap trunks of young trees to prevent sunscald. Put windbreaks and other winter protection in place. Stake newly planted trees. Mulch broad-leaved evergreens. Rake leaves and compost them. Look for overwintering pests; remove and destroy.

Water evergreens deeply before ground freezes. Fertilize deciduous and evergreen trees and shrubs when dormant. Wrap trunks of young trees to prevent sunscald. Put windbreaks and other winter protection in place. Stake newly planted trees. Mulch broad-leaved evergreens. Rake leaves and compost them.

Plant dormant deciduous plants; plant evergreens. Water new plantings and established evergreens deeply. Fertilize deciduous and evergreen trees and shrubs when dormant. Wrap trunks of young trees to prevent sunscald. Begin putting windbreaks in place if needed. Stake newly planted trees. Mulch broad-leaved evergreens. Rake leaves and compost them.

Plant deciduous and evergreen trees and shrubs. Water new plantings deeply. Fertilize established plants when dormant. Wrap trunks of young trees to prevent sunscald. Stake newly planted trees. Take hardwood cuttings when leaves have fallen. Watch for pests and signs of disease.

Plant deciduous and evergreen trees and shrubs. Water new plantings deeply. Fertilize established plants when dormant. Stake newly planted trees. Take hardwood cuttings when leaves have fallen. Watch for pests and signs of disease.

See Zone 9

Roses	Lawns & Ground Covers	Zone
Be sure winter protection is in place: soil mounds, mulch, and protective covers. Remove covers and spray canes with antidesiccant when temperature goes above 40 degrees F if you forgot last month.	Avoid walking on lawn after it freezes, or you may cause bare spots next spring.	*1-3*
Put winter protection in place: soil mounds, mulch when soil freezes, protective covers. Spray canes with antidesiccant before covering plants, when temperature is above 40 degrees F.	See Zone 3	*4*
Mound dirt around base of roses; mulch when soil mound freezes. Spray canes with antidesiccant, when temperature is above 40 degrees F.	Fertilize lawn lightly, after first frost.	*5*
Mound dirt around base of roses. Mulch if desired when soil mound freezes.	See Zone 5	*6*
Do not fertilize roses, even if still blooming. Water deeply if weather is dry. Cut back long canes to prevent wind damage.	Water new plantings if necessary, before ground freezes. Fertilize lawn lightly after first frost.	*7*
Do not fertilize roses, even if still blooming. Water deeply if weather is dry. Cut back long canes to prevent wind damage. Prune off soft, weak growth. Clean up and dispose of dropped leaves.	Plant ground covers and ornamental grasses if weather is still warm. Overseed summer lawns with ryegrass; sow cool-weather lawns, reseed thin or bare spots. Water new plantings regularly if weather is dry. Mow lawn if still necessary. Divide crowded clumps of ornamental grasses.	*8*
Plant dormant roses. Do not fertilize roses again until spring. Water deeply if weather is dry. Cut back long canes to prevent wind damage. Clean up and dispose of dropped leaves.	Plant ground covers and ornamental grasses. Overseed summer lawns with ryegrass; sow cool-weather lawns, reseed thin or bare spots. Water new plantings regularly if weather is dry. Mow lawn if still necessary. Divide crowded clumps of ornamental grasses.	*9*
See Zone 9	See Zone 9	*10-11*

Perennials

Bulbs

	Perennials	Bulbs
1-3	Thickly mulch perennials when ground freezes. Check windbreaks if you need them.	Mulch bulb beds when soil freezes to prevent frost heaving.
4	Thickly mulch perennials when ground freezes. Cut back mums when they finish blooming; mound soil around base of plants to about eight inches high.	Mulch bulb beds when soil freezes to prevent frost heaving. Examine gladiolus corms and throw out old, shriveled, moldy, or damaged ones.
5	Cut back perennials to three to four inches; cut back mums when they finish blooming. Clean up beds and borders. Mulch when ground freezes.	Plant spring bulbs if soil is not yet frozen. When ground freezes, mulch to prevent frost heaving that may expose bulbs. Examine stored gladiolus corms and throw out old, shriveled, moldy, or damaged ones.
6	Cut back perennials to three to four inches; cut back mums when they finish blooming. Clean up beds and borders. Move perennials not reliably hardy into cold frame. Mulch when ground freezes.	Plant spring bulbs before soil freezes. Fertilize at planting. When ground does freeze, mulch if desired to prevent frost heaving that may expose bulbs. Examine stored gladiolus corms and throw out old, shriveled, moldy, or damaged ones.
7	Cut back perennials to three to four inches; cut back mums when they finish blooming. Move perennials not reliably hardy into cold frame. Mulch when ground freezes.	See Zone 6
8	Cut back perennials to two to three inches when they finish blooming. Divide and transplant crowded clumps of perennials; water regularly so plants can establish new roots. Weed and clean up debris from beds and borders.	Dig summer bulbs before first hard frost. Plant precooled spring bulbs (those that have been stored in the refrigerator) before ground freezes. Fertilize at planting. Go through gladiolus corms and throw out old, shriveled, moldy, or damaged ones.
9	Plant new perennials; divide and transplant crowded clumps of spring bloomers. Water new plants regularly. Cut back perennials to two to three inches when topgrowth starts to die back. Weed and clean up debris from beds and borders.	Dig summer bulbs. Plant precooled spring bulbs; fertilize at planting. Go through gladiolus corms and throw out old, shriveled, moldy, or damaged ones.
10-11	See Zone 9	See Zone 9

Annuals

Dig organic matter into beds and borders before soil freezes.

Clean up annuals when frost kills them. Dig organic matter into beds and borders before soil freezes. Mulch hardy annuals sown for spring bloom after first hard frost.

See Zone 5

Clean up annuals when plants stop blooming or are killed by frost. Dig organic matter into beds and borders. Mulch hardy annuals sown for spring bloom after first hard frost.

Plant hardy annuals if weather is still warm. Fertilize annuals already planted for winter bloom; water as necessary.

Plant hardy annuals. Fertilize and pinch back annuals already planted for winter bloom; water as necessary. Pull spent plants. Continue to clean up beds and borders.

See Zone 9

Notes

1-3

Clean out containers and store for winter. Care for tender container plants brought indoors for winter.

Update crop performance records and begin preparing seed orders for spring. Be sure garden is wellp repared for winter, with mulches in place or piled near garden for use when ground freezes.

4

See Zone 3

Update crop performance records. Be sure garden is well-prepared for winter. Mulch perennial herbs when ground freezes.

5

See Zone 3

Harvest late crops from cold frame and garden. Dig root crops or mulch thickly for outdoor storage, and mark with tall stakes. (Carrots, turnips, leeks, and parsnips can be left in the garden under a one-foot-deep layer of mulch and dug as needed all winter.) Dig organic matter into soil before it freezes solid.

6

Clean out containers when late plants finish blooming and late crops stop producing; put contents on compost pile. Care for tender container plants brought indoors for winter.

See Zone 5

7

Clean out containers when late plants finish blooming and late crops stop producing; put contents on compost pile. Care for tender container plants brought indoors for winter. Put marginally hardy container plants in cold frame.

Harvest fall crops. Sow oriental greens and other leafy crops in cold frame. Dig root crops or mulch thickly for outdoor storage. Dig organic matter into soil. Take down trellises and stakes; clean and store for winter.

8

Move marginally hardy container plants into cold frame or sink clay pots into ground. Bring tender plants indoors. Clean out containers when late plants finish blooming and late crops stop producing. Harvest late salad greens still producing.

Harvest fall crops. Sow cool-season crops in garden or cold frame. Protect tender crops from frost. Pull and compost spent crops and weeds not gone to seed. Dig organic matter into soil or plant cover crops in empty parts of garden.

9

Plant hardy annuals in containers. Harvest vegetables and herbs; cut flowers from containers. When plants finish blooming or producing, clean out containers and put contents on compost pile. Watch for pests and signs of disease.

Harvest fall crops. Sow cool-season crops in garden or cold frame. As needed, fertilize, thin, and water crops sown earlier. Pull and compost spent crops and weeds not gone to seed. Dig organic matter into soil or plant cover crops in empty parts of garden.

10-11

See Zone 9

See Zone 9

Fruit

When soil freezes, mulch trees in a ring eight to twelve inches from trunk. Make sure mouse guards, tree wraps, and other winter protection are in place.

See Zone 3

Clean up dropped fruit and leaves. Install mouse guards around tender-barked trees. Wrap trunks of young trees to prevent sunscald. When soil freezes, mulch trees in a ring eight to twelve inches from trunk.

Clean up dropped fruit and leaves. Install mouse guards around tender-barked trees. Wrap trunks of young trees to prevent sunscald. When soil freezes, mulch trees in a ring eight to twelve inches from trunk. Thin and cut back brambles after hard frost. Be sure newly planted trees are securely staked.

Clean up dropped fruit and leaves. Install mouse guards around tender-barked trees. Wrap trunks of young trees to prevent sunscald. Thin and cut back brambles after hard frost. Stake newly planted trees. When soil freezes, mulch trees in a ring eight to twelve inches from trunk.

Plant fruit trees, berries, and grapes if weather still permits. Water new plants deeply; cut back watering of established plants. Clean up dropped fruit and leaves; compost if healthy. Thin and cut back brambles. Stake newly planted trees.

Plant fruit trees, berries, and grapes. Water new plants deeply. Stake newly planted trees. Clean up dropped fruit and leaves; compost if healthy. Thin and cut back brambles.

Plant fruit trees, berries, and grapes. Water new plants deeply. Stake newly planted trees. Clean up dropped fruit and leaves; compost if healthy. Thin and cut back brambles. Watch for pests and signs of disease.

Pruning Diseased Trees and Shrubs

Diseases that are not systemic, including fire blight, canker, and galls, can be halted by pruning away the affected branches or plant parts.

The safest approach is to sterilize cutting tools with rubbing alcohol or bleach solution after each time you cut off a diseased limb. In practice, professionals seldom bother to do this, but if you cut into the diseased portion of the wood it is an appropriate safeguard.

When removing diseased growth, cut back to healthy wood, six or even eight inches below the damaged area.

Do not prune when plants are wet. This applies to healthy as well as diseased trees, shrubs, and vines. Water can carry any disease organisms that might be present right into the newly cut wood.

When you finish pruning, burn or dispose of the diseased cuttings. Do not chip them to use for mulch or put them on the compost pile.

December

As the year draws to a close, gardeners in warm climates are still busy planting winter annuals and harvesting late crops of salad greens and other cool-weather vegetables. But farther north, gardens are at rest until spring. Although winter is the slowest season in the garden, it does not mean there's nothing for gardeners to do. In cold climates, sensitive plants need protection from severe winter conditions. And there are tools to clean and sharpen and the garden journal to update. Then, when seed and nursery catalogs fill the mailbox, it's time to start planning for next year's garden.

Winter Protection for Plants

Winter can be hard on plants in the North, but there are a number of ways you can make conditions less stressful for special plants.

First of all, make sure perennials, shrubs, trees, and woody vines are all well-watered going into winter. When the ground is frozen, plants cannot get water, so it's helpful to make sure their tissues are good and moist when the soil freezes.

For many plants, especially shallow-rooted perennials, the worst winter damage is caused not by the cold, but by winter thaws. Alternate periods of freezing and thawing cause the soil to expand and contract, and plant roots can be forced right out of the ground. When the deep freeze returns, exposed roots will be dehydrated, damaged, or outright killed. A thick mulch of loose material, such as shredded leaves, will help keep the ground frozen during winter warm spells, so roots stay in the ground. Lay the mulch about a foot deep, after the soil has frozen, and leave it in place until the weather moderates in early spring.

Winter mulch can also take the place of an insulating blanket of snow, where there is winter cold but no snow cover to protect delicate alpine plants in rock gardens, roses, and shrubs of borderline hardiness. This kind of mulch is laid earlier, before the soil freezes solid, and keeps the ground from freezing as deeply as it would if left unprotected. You can also mulch carrots, parsnips, and some other root vegetables in this way, and leave them in the garden all winter, to dig whenever you want them.

Roses, especially hybrid teas and grandifloras, benefit from winter protection in climates where winter temperatures are likely to drop below 20 degrees F often or for extended periods. Good growing practices help prepare roses for winter cold. New growth is most susceptible to damage, so stop fertilizing six to eight weeks before you expect the first frost, and don't prune late in the season. Pruning, like fertilizing, stimulates new growth.

To protect individual plants in climates where the temperature seldom goes below zero, mound up soil to a height of eight to twelve inches around the base of each plant. (Bring the soil from an empty part of the garden; do not take it from the rose bed.)

In colder areas, top the soil mound with about a foot of loose mulch when the mound freezes. Hold the mulch in place with a cylinder of chicken wire or hardware cloth. In the very coldest places, where temperatures may plunge below -15 degrees F for any length of time, enclose rose bushes completely by putting caps, cones, baskets, or other covers over them, on top of the soil mound and mulch. Remove or open the covers on warm days to let in fresh air.

In fall, after the first few frosts but before the ground freezes solid, prune the canes of bush roses to half their length, tie them loosely together with twine, and make the soil mounds. When the mounds freeze, add the mulch and, if necessary, the covers.

Climbing roses need protection, too. Detach the canes from their trellis, bend them carefully to the ground, and peg them down. Cover the canes with soil, and when that freezes, cover with a layer of mulch. Hold the mulch in place by covering it with chicken wire or burlap weighted down at the corners.

When winter cold begins to give way to warmer spring weather, remove the caps and start removing the loose mulch, a little at a time. Leave the soil mound in place until the danger of heavy frost is past, then gradually remove it, too. If possible, remove mulches and mounds on cloudy days, so the newly exposed canes will not suffer sunburn.

The cold winds of winter can quickly dry out plants, causing their tissues to suffer damage from windburn. If your garden location is exposed to frequent strong winds, it would be advisable to plant a windbreak of tall evergreen shrubs on the side of your property from which the prevailing winter winds blow. You can also spray broadleaved evergreens and other flowering shrubs with an antidesiccant. Apply the spray in late fall and early spring, and once or more during the winter if the temperature goes above 40 degrees F.

Construct little shelters around sensitive shrubs to protect them from ice and snow buildup, and also from windburn. You can wrap shrubs for the winter in burlap or chicken wire to hold the branches upright, or make a screen for a group of shrubs by stretching burlap around wooden stakes driven into the ground. For foun-

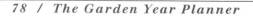

dation shrubs growing under rain gutters, where melting snow can drip onto them and form ice, the best way to protect the plants is to build a roofed shelter of scrap lumber that will cover them like a little house. Next year, consider moving the plants to a less difficult location.

Where the winter sun can be bright but followed by bitterly cold nights, young trees are at risk of sunscald. Sunscald occurs when the tree tissues thaw and warm on a sunny day, then refreeze at night; the expansion cracks the bark. This can occur in urban areas, where buildings and pavements reflect heat that warms plants on sunny days. To prevent sunscald, wrap the trunks of young trees with tree wrap from right under the lowest branches all the way to the ground. Mulch helps, too.

Updating Garden Plans

Cold winter evenings are the perfect time to assess the successes and failures of this year's garden, and to plan ahead for next year. Seed and nursery catalogs start arriving before Christmas, and you will want to place your orders as soon as possible after the holidays to get the best selection, especially if you are ordering new or rare plants of which the commercial stock is small.

Keeping a garden journal is an immense help in planning for the future. A journal allows you to acquire a good understanding of your plants and your garden over time, as you record seed starting, transplanting, blooming, and harvest times; first and last frost dates; weather conditions; and how plants fared in the garden. A journal also lets you remember the special enjoyment of the year's first snowdrop, the day you saw an indigo bunting at the bird feeder, and the night the first moonflowers bloomed. There are so many special moments in a garden, and keeping a journal lets you hold onto them.

In winter, as you plan the changes you want to make in next year's garden, and dream about the plants you want to add, you can look back over your journals from past gardening seasons and see how far you've come.

Check winter protection for shrubs and trees to make sure it is secure; check mouse guards and windbreaks. Look for overwintering pests; remove and destroy. Start planning spring plant orders.

1-3

See Zone 3

4

Put windbreaks, mouse guards, and other winter protection in place. When soil freezes a few inches deep, mulch new plants. Look for overwintering pests; remove and destroy. Start planning spring plant orders.

5

See Zone 5

6

Water evergreens deeply before ground freezes. Put windbreaks, mouse guards, and other winter protection in place. When soil freezes a few inches deep, mulch new plants. Look for overwintering pests; remove and destroy. Start planning spring plant orders.

7

Finish planting bare-root stock if soil is not frozen. Water evergreens and new plants deeply before ground freezes. Put windbreaks, mouse guards, and other winter protection in place if needed. When soil freezes a few inches deep, mulch new plants. Look for overwintering pests; remove and destroy. Start planning spring plant orders.

8

Finish planting bare-root stock and evergreens. Water and fertilize newly planted stock. Prune established trees, shrubs, and vines while dormant; prune any frost-damaged growth from tropical plants. Take hardwood cuttings. Watch for pests and signs of disease. Start planning spring plant orders.

9

Finish planting bare-root stock and evergreens. Water and fertilize newly planted stock. Prune established trees, shrubs, and vines while dormant. Take hardwood cuttings. Watch for pests and signs of disease. Start planning spring plant orders.

10-11

Roses

Lawns & Ground Covers

1-3

Check winter protection periodically to be sure it stays in place. Start planning spring plant orders.

Try not to walk on lawn when it is frozen, or you may cause bare spots next spring.

4

Put protective covers in place if not yet done. Check winter protection periodically to be sure it stays in place. Start planning spring plant orders.

See Zone 3

5

When protective soil mounds have frozen, top with mulch. Check winter protection periodically to be sure it stays in place. Start planning spring plant orders.

See Zone 3

6

See Zone 5

See Zone 3

7

Mound soil around base of individual plants. Start planning spring plant orders.

Rake up leaves from lawns, especially new ones. When ground freezes, try not to walk on lawn.

8

Prune off any soft, weak late growth. Clean up and dispose of dropped leaves. Mound soil around base of individual plants. Start planning spring plant orders.

See Zone 7

9

Plant bare-root roses while dormant. Fertilize new plants and water regularly. Check to make sure climbers stay fastened to their supports. Clean up and dispose of any dropped leaves. Start planning spring plant orders.

Lightly fertilize or top-dress with compost new cool-season lawns, and ryegrass sown over summer lawns. Water if weather is dry.

10-11

See Zone 9

See Zone 9

Periodically check mulched perennials for frost heaving if there is no snow cover. Check windbreaks and other winter protection. Update designs for beds and borders; start planning spring plant orders.

See Zone 3

When ground freezes, mulch perennials to prevent frost heaving. Update designs for beds and borders; start planning spring plant orders.

See Zone 5

See Zone 5

Mulch perennials after first hard freeze. Protect tender plants when threatened by a freeze. Weed and clean up beds and borders. Update designs for beds and borders; start planning spring plant orders.

Plant perennials. Water new plants regularly. Protect tender plants when threatened by a freeze. Weed and clean up beds and borders. Update designs for beds and borders; start planning spring plant orders.

Plant perennials. Water new plants regularly. Weed and clean up debris from beds and borders. Update designs for beds and borders; start planning spring plant orders.

	Bulbs	Annuals
1-3	Mulch bulbs planted in fall with leaves or evergreen boughs. Check summer bulbs in storage; throw out any with mold, mildew, or soft spots.	Update designs for beds and borders; start planning seed and plant orders for spring.
4	See Zone 3	See Zone 3
5	See Zone 3	Care for plants growing indoors from cuttings taken in fall. Update designs for beds and borders; start planning seed and plant orders for spring.
6	Mulch bulbs planted in fall with leaves or evergreen boughs when ground freezes. Check summer bulbs in storage; throw out any with mold, mildew, or soft spots.	See Zone 5
7	See Zone 6	Care for plants growing indoors from cuttings taken in fall. Clean up gardens if not yet done. Update designs for beds and borders; start planning seed and plant orders for spring.
8	Finish planting precooled spring bulbs. Mulch after first hard freeze with leaves or evergreen boughs. Check summer bulbs in storage; throw out any with mold, mildew, or soft spots.	Weed, water, fertilize, and deadhead winter annuals. Update designs for next year's beds and borders; start planning seed and plant orders for spring.
9	Plant precooled spring bulbs; fertilize at planting. Water if weather is dry.	Plant hardy annuals. Weed, water, fertilize, and deadhead plants already growing. Pull fall plants when worn-out. Update designs for next year's beds and borders; start planning seed and plant orders for spring.
10-11	See Zone 9	See Zone 9

Container Gardens	Vegetables & Herbs	
Care for tender container plants brought indoors for winter. Start planning container plantings for next year; begin preparing seed and plant orders.	Check windbreaks, mulches, and other winter protection. Update garden designs; begin preparing seed and plant orders for spring. Plan ahead to order seeds for starting indoors.	*1-3*
See Zone 3	See Zone 3	*4*
See Zone 3	Dig root crops stored in garden under mulch as needed. Check windbreaks, mulches, and other winter protection. Update garden designs; begin preparing seed and plant orders for spring. Plan ahead to order seeds for starting indoors.	*5*
See Zone 3	Dig root crops stored in garden under mulch as needed. Harvest late crops from cold frame. Ventilate cold frame on warm days. Check windbreaks, mulches, and other winter protection. Mulch garden when ground is frozen. Update garden designs; begin preparing seed and plant orders for spring.	*6*
Clean out any containers still in need of it. Care for tender container plants brought indoors for winter. Check container plants in cold frame periodically. Start planning container plantings for next year; begin preparing seed and plant orders.	See Zone 6	*7*
See Zone 7	Harvest late crops from garden and cold frame. Plant cool-weather leafy greens in cold frame. Ventilate cold frame on warm days. Mulch root crops stored in garden. Clean up empty parts of garden. Update garden designs; begin preparing seed and plant orders for spring.	*8*
Harvest late vegetables in containers. Care for winter annuals and other container plants. Watch for pests and signs of disease. Start planning container plantings for next year; begin preparing seed and plant orders.	Harvest crops from garden and cold frame. Plant cool-weather crops in garden or cold frame. Ventilate cold frame on warm days. Clean up empty parts of garden. Dig organic matter into soil or plant cover crops. Update garden designs; begin preparing seed and plant orders for spring.	*9*
See Zone 9	Harvest crops as they become ready. Plant cool-weather crops. Fertilize, thin, and water crops sown earlier. Clean up empty parts of garden. Dig organic matter into soil or plant cover crops. Update garden designs; begin preparing seed and plant orders for spring.	*10-11*

1-3

Check mouse guards, mulches, and other winter protection. Begin planning nursery orders for spring.

4

Check mouse guards, mulches, and other winter protection. Start planning nursery orders for spring. Sharpen pruning tools in a preparation for dormant pruning. Check for overwintering pests; remove and destroy.

5

See Zone 4

6

Install mouse guards and other winter protection if not yet done. Start planning nursery orders for spring. Sharpen pruning tools in preparation for dormant pruning. Check for overwintering pests; remove and destroy.

7

Install mouse guards and other winter protection if not yet done. When soil freezes, mulch trees in a ring eight to twelve inches from trunk. Clean up dropped fruit and leaves. Start planning nursery orders for spring. Sharpen pruning tools in preparation for dormant pruning. Check for overwintering pests; remove and destroy.

8

Plant bare-root stock if soil is still workable. Water new plants deeply. Prune established fruit trees, bushes, and grapevines when leaves are gone. Clean up dropped fruit and leaves. Plan nursery orders for spring. Sharpen pruning tools in preparation for dormant pruning. Check for overwintering pests; remove and destroy.

9

Plant fruit trees, berries, and grapes. Water new plants deeply. Stake newly planted trees. Set up heaters for citrus if a freeze is expected. Clean up dropped fruit and leaves. Prune trees and bushes while dormant. Check for overwintering pests; remove and destroy. Apply dormant oil sprays.

10-11

Plant fruit trees, berries, and grapes. Water new plants deeply. Stake newly planted trees. Clean up dropped fruit and leaves. Prune trees and bushes while dormant. Check for pests and diseases. Apply dormant oil sprays.

Tool Maintenance

Keeping your garden tools in good shape will extend their life, and also make them more enjoyable to use and more effective. Dull pruning shears are hard to use and they can crush branches instead of cutting cleanly through them.

Clean caked-on dirt from shovels, spades, and trowels. Sharpen the edges of dull blades with a file. Wipe the blades with an oily rag or dip them into a bucket of oily sand. Wipe wooden handles with an oily rag, then a clean rag.

Clean grass from the lawn mower, especially the underside. If the mower is several years old, a change of spark plugs or a professional cleaning and tune-up service might also be in order.

Have pruning shears and lawn mower blades sharpened professionally. If you have trees and shrubs in need of pruning this year, remember that late winter is the best time to prune many of them, so have your shears, saws, and lopers ready to go.

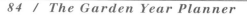

Appendixes

Plants for Shady Gardens

The plants listed below tolerate varying degrees of shade.

ANNUALS
Anchusa
Begonia, wax begonia
Browallia
Calendula, pot marigold
Callistephus, China aster
Cleome, spider flower
Coleus
Euphorbia
Fuchsia
Impatiens
Lobelia
Lobularia, sweet alyssum
Lunaria, money plant
Myosotis, forget-me-not
Nicotiana
Nierembergia, cup flower
Thunbergia, clock vine, black-eyed Susan vine
Torenia, wishbone flower
Verbena

BULBS
Caladium
Chionodoxa, glory-of-the-snow
Colchicum, autumn crocus
Convallaria, lily-of-the-valley
Crocus (need sun when blooming)
Endymion, Spanish bluebell
Eranthis, winter aconite
Galanthus, snowdrop
Iris, crested iris
Leucojum, snowflake
Lilium, lily
Lycoris, magic lily
Narcissus, daffodil and narcissus
Scilla, Siberian squill

ORNAMENTAL GRASSES AND GROUND COVERS
Ajuga, bugleweed
Arundinaria, bamboo
Asarum, European wild ginger
Ceratostigma, plumbago
Epimedium
Euonymus, wintercreeper
Galium, sweet woodruff
Hedera, ivy
Helictotrichon, blue oat grass
Lamium
Liriope, lilyturf
Miscanthus, fountain grass
Ophiopogon, mondo grass
Pachysandra
Phalaris, ribbon grass
Vinca, periwinkle

PERENNIALS AND BIENNIALS
Aegopodium, goutweed
Alchemilla, lady's mantle
Amsonia, blue star
Anemone
Arum
Aruncus, goatsbeard
Astilbe
Athyrium, Japanese silver fern
Bergenia
Brunnera, Siberian bugloss
Chelone, turtlehead
Cimicifuga, black snakeroot
Cyclamen
Dennstaedtia, hay-scented fern
Dicentra, bleeding heart
Digitalis, foxglove
Eupatorium, hardy ageratum
Euphorbia, spurge
Filipendula, meadowsweet
Geranium, cranesbill
Helleborus, Christmas rose, Lenten rose
Hemerocallis, day lily
Hosta
Lysimachia, loosestrife
Mertensia, Virginia bluebell
Monarda, bee balm

Osmunda, cinnamon fern, royal fern
Paeonia, peony
Phlox, creeping phlox
Physostegia, false dragonhead
Platycodon, balloon flower
Polygonatum, Solomon's seal
Polystichum, Christmas fern
Pulmonaria, lungwort
Sedum
Tiarella, foamflower
Veronica, speedwell
Viola

TREES, SHRUBS, AND VINES
Abelia
Acer palmatum, Japanese cut-leaf maple
Azalea
Buxus, box
Calycanthus, sweet shrub
Cephalotaxus, plum-yew
Chimonanthus, winter sweet
Clematis
Clethra, sweet pepper bush
Corylopsis, winter hazel
Cornus, dogwood
Daphne
Deutzia
Enkianthus
Euonymus, burning bush
Fothergilla
Hamamelis, witch hazel
Hydrangea: climbing, lace cap, oak leaf hydrangeas
Ilex, Japanese holly
Kalmia, mountain laurel
Kerria
Ligustrum, privet
Philadelphus, mock orange
Pieris, Japanese andromeda
Rhododendron, rhododendron
Skimmia
Taxus, yew
Tsuga, hemlock
Vaccinium, blueberry

Arugula
Asparagus
Bee balm
Beets
Borage
Broccoli
Cabbage
Carrots
Chard
Chervil
Chinese cabbage
Chives
Coriander
Corn salad
Cress
Endive and escarole
Hyssop
Kale
Leaf lettuce
Mints
Mustard
Bunching onions, scallions
Parsley
Peas
Radishes
Sage
Sorrel
Spinach
Tarragon

Cutting Flowers

Achillea, yarrow
Agapanthus
Ageratum
Alcea, hollyhock
Alchemilla, lady's-mantle
Alstroemeria
Anaphalis, pearly everlasting
Anemone
Anthemis, golden marguerite
Antirrhinum, snapdragon
Aquilegia, columbine
Armeria, thrift
Asclepias, butterfly weed
Aster
Astilbe
Bellis, English daisy
Bergenia

Brunnera, Siberian bugloss
Dahlia
Delphinium
Dianthus, garden pinks
Digitalis, foxglove
Echinacea, purple coneflower
Eremurus, foxtail lily
Eschscholzia, California poppy
Eustoma, Lisianthus
Freesia
Gaillardia, blanketflower
Gazania
Gerbera
Geum
Gladiolus
Gomphrena, globe amaranth
Gypsophila, baby's breath
Helenium, sneezeweed
Helianthus, sunflower
Helichrysum, strawflower
Heliopsis, sunflower
Heliotropium, heliotrope
Hemerocallis, day lily
Heuchera, coralbells
Hyacinthus, hyacinth
Hydrangea
Iberis, globe candytuft
Iris
Kniphofia, red-hot poker
Lathyrus, sweet pea
Lavandula, lavender
Liatris, gayfeather
Lilium, lily
Limonium, statice
Lobularia, sweet alyssum
Lunaria, money plant
Lupinus, lupine
Lysimachia, loosestrife
Matthiola, stock
Molucella, bells of Ireland
Monarda, bee balm
Muscari, grape hyacinth
Myosotis, forget-me-not
Narcissus, daffodil
Nicotiana
Nigella, love-in-a-mist
Ornithogalum, star-of-Bethlehem
Paeonia, peony
Papaver, poppy
Pelargonium, geranium
Penstemon

Petunia
Phlox
Physalis, Chinese lantern
Physostegia, false dragonhead
Platycodon, balloon flower
Polianthes, tuberose
Ranunculus, Persian buttercup
Reseda, mignonette
Rosa, rose
Rudbeckia, black-eyed Susan, gloriosa daisy
Salpiglossis, painted tongue
Salvia
Scabiosa, pincushion flower
Schizanthus, butterfly flower
Solidago, goldenrod
Syringa, lilac
Tagetes, marigold
Torenia, wishbone flower
Trachymene, blue lace flower
Trollius, globeflower
Tropaeolum, nasturtium
Tulipa, tulip
Verbena
Veronica
Viburnum
Viola, pansy, violet
Zantedeschia, calla lily
Zinnia

Fragrant Flowers and Plants

Basil (leaves)
Dianthus, garden pinks
Lavender (flowers and leaves)
Lilium, lily
Lobularia, sweet alyssum
Marjoram, (leaves)
Monarda, bee balm
Nepeta, catmint (leaves)
Nicotiana alata
Oregano (leaves)
Paeonia, peony
Petunia
Phlox, garden phlox
Rose
Rosemary (leaves)
Thyme (leaves)
Tropaeolum, nasturtium

Slow-Growing Annuals

These plants need to be started indoors at least 10 weeks before the last spring frost.

Begonia
Catharanthus, Madagascar peri-
  winkle
Exacum, Persian violet
Heliotropium, heliotrope
Hypoestes, polka-dot plant
Impatiens
Lobelia
Mimulus, monkey flower
Pelargonium, geranium
Petunia
Torenia, wishbone flower
Verbena

Temperature Needs of Annuals

Numbers following plant names refer to the number of weeks before the last frost date to sow seeds indoors.

Can tolerate a fair amount of frost, and grow best in cool weather. Direct-sow in fall, or in spring as soon as soil can be worked, unless otherwise noted.

Calendula, pot marigold
Centaurea, bachelor's button,
  basket flower
Cleome: four weeks; seeds may
  be damaged by frost
Consolida, larkspur
Coreopsis: 6 weeks, or direct-
  sow
Cynoglossum, Chinese forget-me-
  not: 6 weeks, or direct-sow
Dyssodia, Dahlberg daisy: 8
  weeks, or direct-sow
Eschscholzia, California poppy
Gaillardia, blanketflower: 4
  weeks, or direct-sow
Helianthus, sunflower

Iberis, globe candytuft
Lathyrus, sweet pea
Linaria, toadflax
Lobularia, sweet alyssum
Lupinus, annual lupine: 4 weeks
Myosotis, annual forget-me-not
Nigella, love-in-a-mist
Papaver, field poppy
Rudbeckia, black-eyed Susan,
  gloriosa daisy

Tolerate occasional light frost, but are killed by prolonged cold. Plant out when danger of frost is past, or direct-sow when soil is workable and last hard frost is past.

Antirrhinum, snapdragon: 8
  weeks
Brachycome, Swan River daisy: 6
  weeks
Callistephus, China aster: 6
  weeks
Celosia: 4 weeks
Chrysanthemum, annual types: 6
  weeks
Dianthus chinensis, China pink:
  6 to 8 weeks
Eustoma, lisianthus: 8 weeks
Felicia, blue marguerite, 6 to 8
  weeks
Gazania: 4 weeks
Gerbera: 8 weeks
Gomphrena, globe amaranth: 6
  weeks
Helichrysum, strawflower: 6
  weeks
Lobelia: 10 weeks
Matthiola, stock: 6 weeks
Mirabilis, four o'clock: 6 weeks
Molucella, bells of Ireland: 6 to 8
  weeks
Nemesia: 8 weeks
Nicotiana: 6 weeks
Nierembergia, cupflower: 6
  weeks
Petunia: 10 weeks
Phlox: 6 to 8 weeks
Portulaca: 6 weeks
Salvia: 8 weeks
Scabiosa, pincushion flower: 6 to
  8 weeks

Schizanthus, butterfly flower: 8
  weeks
Tagetes, marigold: 8 weeks
Torenia, wishbone flower: 10
  weeks
Trachymene, blue lace flower: 8
  weeks
Verbena: 12 weeks
Viola, pansy: 12 weeks
Zinnia: 6 weeks

Cannot tolerate frost; need warm soil and warm weather.

Ageratum: 8 weeks
Begonia: 12 to 16 weeks
Browallia: 8 weeks
Catharanthus, Madagascar peri-
  winkle: 12 weeks
Coleus: 8 weeks
Cosmos: 4 weeks
Dahlia: 8 weeks
Exacum, Persian violet: 10 to 12
  weeks
Heliotropium, heliotrope: 12
  weeks
Hypoestes, polka-dot plant: 12
  weeks
Impatiens: 10 weeks
Ipomoea, morning glory: direct-
  sow
Mimulus, monkey flower: 10
  weeks
Pelargonium, geranium: 10
  weeks
Salpiglossis, painted tongue: 8
  weeks
Thunbergia, clock vine, black-
  eyed Susan vine: 6 weeks
Tropaeolum, nasturtium: direct-
  sow

Temperature Needs of Vegetables and Herbs

Arugula
Asparagus
Broccoli
Brussels sprouts
Cabbage

Cauliflower
Celeriac
Chervil
Chinese cabbage
Corn salad (mache)
Cress
Garlic
Kale
Lettuce
Mustard greens
Onions
Parsley
Peas
Radishes
Shallots
Spinach
Turnips

WARM-WEATHER
Basil
Lima beans
Snap and shell beans
Coriander
Corn
Cucumbers
Dill
Eggplant
Marjoram
Okra
Peppers
Rosemary
Sage
Squash
Tarragon
Thyme
Tomatoes

Bulb-Planting Depths

Anemone: two inches
Tuberous begonia: just below
  soil surface
Caladium: just below soil surface

Calla lily: three to four inches
Canna: two to three inches
Colchicum: three inches
Crocus: two to three inches
Cyclamen: one to two inches
Dahlia: four inches
Freesia: four inches
Fritillaria: five inches
Gladiolus: four to seven inches,
  depending on size
Grape hyacinth: three to four
  inches
Hyacinth: four inches
Bearded iris: just below soil sur-
  face
Dutch iris: four inches
Lily: five to eight inches,
  depending on size
Lily-of-the-valley: two inches
Narcissus: five inches
Ranunculus: two inches
Snowdrop: two to three inches
Squill: three inches
Tulip: five to seven inches

Plants for Acid Soil

TREES AND SHRUBS
Abies, fir
Arctostaphylos, bearberry
Azalea
Calluna, heather
Camellia
Clethra, sweet pepper bush
Enkianthus
Erica, heath
Gardenia
Gaultheria, wintergreen
Ilex, holly
Kalmia, mountain laurel
Leucothoe
Magnolia, sweet bay magnolia
Myrica, bayberry
Pieris, andromeda

Pinus, pine
Quercus, oak
Rhododendron
Vaccinium, blueberry

PERENNIALS
Chelone, turtlehead
Cimicifuga, black snakeroot
Dicentra, fringed bleeding heart
Digitalis, foxglove
Mertensia, Virginia bluebell
Trillium

Winter-Blooming Flowers

The following plants bloom in winter to early spring, depending on location.

Abeliophyllum
Adonis
Anemone, Grecian windflower
Bulbocodium, meadow saffron
Camellia
Chimonanthus, winter sweet
Chionodoxa, glory-of-the-snow
Corylopsis, winter hazel
Crocus, early species
Daphne
Eranthis, winter aconite
Erica, winter heath
Galanthus, snowdrop
Hamamelis, witch hazel
Helleborus, Christmas rose
Iris, netted iris, Dutch iris
Jasminum, winter jasmine
Lonicera, winter honeysuckle
Narcissus, February Gold, Feb-
  ruary Silver, Paperwhite
Primula, primrose
Salix, pussy willow
Scilla, Persian squill

Sources of Seeds, Plants, and Supplies

<u>SEEDS AND PLANTS</u>

Abbey Gardens
4620 Carpenteria Avenue
Carpenteria, CA 93013

Abundant Life Seed Foundation
P.O. Box 772
Port Townsend, WA 98368

Bear Creek Nursery
P.O. Box 411
Northport, WA 99157
  Fruit trees

Bernardo Beach Native Plant
  Farm
Star Route 7, Box 145
Veguita, NM 87062

Bluestone Perennials
7211 Middle Ridge Road
Madison, OH 44057

Bountiful Gardens
Ecology Action
5798 Ridgewood Road
Willits, CA 95490

Breck's
6523 North Galena Road
Peoria, IL 61632
  Bulbs

Lee Bristol Nursery
R.R. 1, Box 148
Gaylordsville, CT 06755
  Day lilies

W. Atlee Burpee & Co.
Warminster, PA 18974

Carroll Gardens
P.O. Box 310
Westminster, MD 21157

Comstock, Ferre and Co.
Box 125
263 Main Street
Wethersfield, CT 06109

The Cook's Garden
P.O. Box 535
Londonderry, VT 05148

The Country Garden
Route 2, Box 455A
Crivitz, WI 54114

DeGiorgi Company Inc.
6011 M Street
Omaha, NE 68117

Dogwood Hills Nursery
Route 3, Box 181
Franklinton, LA 70438

Henry Field Seed and Nursery Co.
407 Sycamore Street
Shenandoah, IA 51602

Forest Farm
990 Tetherow Road
Williams, OR 97544

The Fragrant Path
P.O. Box 328
Fort Calhoun, NE 68023

Garden Place
P.O. Box 388
Mentor, OH 44061

Harris Seeds
961 Lyell Avenue
Rochester, NY 14606

Holbrook Farm & Nursery
Route 2, Box 223
Fletcher, NC 28732

J. L. Hudson, Seedsman
P.O. Box 1058
Redwood City, CA 94064

Jackson & Perkins Co.
P.O. Box 1028
Medford, OR 97501

Le Jardin du Gourmet
P.O. Box 75
St. Johnsbury Center, VT 05863

Johnny's Selected Seeds
P.O. Box 2580
Albion, ME 04910

Klehm Nursery
Route 5, 197 Penny Road
South Barrington, IL 60010

McClure Zimmerman
P.O. Box 368
Friesland, WI 53935
  Bulbs

Milaeger's Gardens
4838 Douglas Avenue
Racine, WI 53402

Nichols Garden Nursery
1190 North Pacific Highway
Albany, OR 97321

Park Seed Co.
Cokesbury Road
Greenwood, SC 29647

Pinetree Garden Seeds
New Gloucester, ME 04260

Plants of the Southwest
1812 Second Street
Santa Fe, NM 87501

Rex Bulb Farms
P.O. Box 774
Port Townsend, WA 98368

John Scheepers, Inc
RD 6, Phillipsburg Road
Middletown, NY 10940
  Bulbs

Seeds Blum
Idaho City Stage
Boise, ID 83706

Shepherd's Garden Seeds
30 Irene Street
Torrington, CT 06790

Spring Hill Nurseries Co.
6523 North Galena Road
Peoria, IL 61632

Stokes Seeds, Inc.
Box 548
Buffalo, NY 14240

Thompson & Morgan
P.O. Box 1308
Jackson, NJ 08527

Van Bourgondien Bros.
Route 109, 245 Farmingdale
Road
Babylon, NY 11702

Andre Viette Farm & Nursery
Route 1, Box 16
Fishersville, VA 22939

Wayside Gardens
Hodges, SC 29695

Well-Sweep Herb Farm
317 Mt. Bethel Road
Port Murray, NJ 07865

White Flower Farm
Litchfield, CT 06759

TOOLS, EQUIPMENT, AND SUPPLIES

Gardener's Supply
128 Intervale Road
Burlington, VT 05401

Gardens Alive!
Natural Gardening Research
Center
P.O. Box 149, Highway 48
Sunman, IN 46041

The Kinsman Company
River Road
Point Pleasant, PA 18950

The Natural Gardening Company
217 San Anselmo Avenue
San Anselmo, CA 94960

The Necessary Catalog
8320 Salem Avenue
New Castle, VA 24127

Walt Nicke Co.
P.O. Box 433
36 McLeod Lane
Topsfield, MA 01983

Ringer
9959 Valley View Road
Eden Prairie, MN 55344

Recommended Reading

Clausen, Ruth Rogers, and Nicolas H. Ekstrom, *Perennials for American Gardens.* New York: Random House, 1989

Halpin, Anne, *Great Gardens from Everyday Plants.* New York: Fireside Books, 1993

Harper, Pamela J., *Designing with Perennials.* New York: Macmillan Publishing Co., 1991

Heriteau, Jacqueline, *The American Horticultural Society Flower Finder.* New York: Simon & Schuster, 1992

Hill, Lewis, *Pruning Simplified.* Emmaus, PA: Rodale Press, Inc., Out of print—check local libraries for a copy.

Johnson, Hugh, *The Principles of Gardening.* New York: Fireside Books, 1979

Loewer, Peter, *Rodale's Annual Garden.* New York: Wings Books (Random House/Outlet), 1992

Loewer, Peter, *Tough Plants for Tough Places.* Emmaus, PA: Rodale Press, Inc., 1992

McGourty, Frederick, *The Perennial Gardener.* Boston: Houghton Mifflin Co., 1989

Plants and Gardens (handbook series). Brooklyn, NY: Brooklyn Botanic Garden, ongoing

Rodale's Illustrated Encyclopedia of Herbs. Emmaus, PA: Rodale Press, Inc., 1987

Taylor's Guide to Annuals. Boston: Houghton Mifflin Co., 1986. Part of an ongoing series which includes guides on bulbs, herbs, and perennials.

Wyman, Donald. *Wyman's Gardening Encyclopedia.* New York: Macmillan Publishing Co., 1987

Index